THE FURNITURE OF ROBERT ADAM

THE FURNITURE

OF

ROBERT ADAM

EILEEN HARRIS

PH.D. (COLUMBIA UNIVERSITY)

ACADEMY EDITIONS · LONDON

ST. MARTIN'S PRESS · NEW YORK

First published in Great Britain by Alec Tiranti Ltd. in 1963
as number 38 in the series *Chapters in Art*

This edition first published in Great Britain in 1973
by Academy Editions 7 Holland Street London W8

This edition first published in the U.S.A. in 1973 by
St. Martin's Press Inc. 175 Fifth Avenue New York N.Y. 10010
Affiliated publishers: Macmillan Limited, London also at
Bombay, Calcutta, Madras and Melbourne

Printed and bound in Great Britain by Suttons (Paignton) Ltd.
and at The Pitman Press, Bath

TO MY PARENTS

CONTENTS

ACKNOWLEDGEMENTS

In preparing this book I have received the advice and assistance of many individuals. I am firstly indebted to Miss Dorothy Stroud and Sir John Summerson for making the Adam drawings in the Soane Museum available to me on countless occasions. Without their co-operation, my work would not have been possible. My greatest thanks are due to Mr. F. J. B. Watson, who has generously imparted much of his valuable time and expert knowledge, who has read my text with improving results, and whose book on Louis XVI furniture has been a constant source of inspiration. Long discussions and correspondence with Mr. Svend Eriksen have contributed a great deal to my understanding of early Neo-classicism.

I am especially grateful to Mr. Lionel Bell for handling with skill and patience my complicated requests for photography. Mr. Cecil Farthing and the staff of the National Buildings Record have also been of great assistance with illustrations; and Mr. Leslie Harris has been kind enough to lend me several of his superb slides.

I wish to express my gratitude to all of the owners and curators who have allowed me to examine their furniture, supplied me with information and photographs, and permitted me to publish them: to Mr. H. D. Molesworth of the Victoria and Albert Museum, Mr. James Parker of the Metropolitan Museum, Mr. David Du Bon of the Philadelphia Museum, Mr. T. H. Lunsingh-Scheuleer of the Rijksmuseum, and Mr. P. J. Barlow of the National Museum of Wales. Among the private owners I would like to thank His Grace the Duke of Northumberland, the Marquis of Lansdowne, the Earl of Harewood, Earl Spencer, Viscount Scarsdale, Lord Methuen, Lord St. Oswald,

Sir Harold Wernher, the Hon. Andrew Vanneck, Dr. Campbell Golding, and Mrs. Ellery Sedgwick.

I am pleased to acknowledge Miss Elizabeth Aslin, H. Blairman & Sons, Lord Brabourne, Mr. I. O. Chance, Mr. G. L. Conran, Mr. J. Edwards, Mr. John Fleming, Mr. Rupert Gunnis, M. Harris, Ltd., Mr. J. R. Hickish, Mr. A. G. Lewis, Mallett & Son, Miss Elizabeth Murdock, Mr. N. M. Neatby, Frank Partridge & Sons, Mr. Richard Timewell, Mr. Urwick-Smith, Mr. B. Weinreb, and Mr. J. R. Whitfield for their help with various matters.

Finally, to my husband goes my deepest gratitude for his endless patience, encouragement, and guidance throughout the preparation of this book.

PHOTOGRAPHS

British Museum fig. 2; Christie's Ltd. fig. 8; Dr. Campbell Golding fig. 133; Leslie Harris Esq. figs. 1,4,35,107,151; M. Harris Ltd. fig. 37; London County Council fig. 58; Mallett & Son Ltd. figs. 89,149; Metropolitan Museum of Art, New York figs. 38,153; National Buildings Record figs. 9–13,15,16,24,26–30,32, 53–56,65,70,71,74,96,101,132,137,141,142,145,147; National Building Trust figs. 21,22,36; National Museum of Wales fig. 25; Frank Partridge Ltd. fig. 123; Philadelphia Museum of Art figs. 100,105,130; Rijksmuseum, Amsterdam fig. 146; Mrs. Ellery Sedgwick fig. 19; Sotheby's fig. 103; Taylor & Dull fig. 104; Victoria & Albert Museum figs. 6,41,45,46,86,98,102,106,108,109,117,120,121, 128,131,138,139,144,155; Wernher Collection fig. 20.

PREFACE

Although for the past century Adam's name has been universally employed to describe an entire period, and an infinite quantity of English furniture, oddly enough, no attempt has yet been made to examine fully the works, or to define the style that made him so famous. This lacuna in the history of furniture is even more amazing in view of the unique opportunities afforded by the collection of Adam drawings preserved in Sir John Soane's Museum. Here lies the whole story of Robert Adam's furniture, more or less untapped.

To deal with all of the many objects which might be classified as furniture or furnishings would demand a volume considerably larger, and more costly than the present one. A certain degree of selection has therefore been necessary. Carpets, better studied in conjunction with ceiling designs; bookcases (except when free standing), and organs —both conceived essentially as architectural units; plate, clocks, and other accessories; chandeliers; curtain cornices; door furniture and fireplace fittings have all been excluded. My study is focussed upon tables, cabinets and commodes, mirrors, girandoles, seat furniture, beds, and pedestals.

From the existing designs, pieces, accounts and biographical data, I have attempted to present a coherent account of the origin, development, and character of Adam furniture. Although I have restricted myself to documented Adam works, I have, wherever appropriate, included pieces by other designers both as a foil to heighten the distinguishing characteristics of Adam's style, and as an illustration of its sources or influences. Since Adam was a designer and not a maker of furniture, much more attention is devoted to the elements of design which identify his works, than to the less significant factors of craftsmanship.

I hope that my efforts will impart an accurate, and justly proportioned picture of Robert Adam's place in the history of English and French Neo-classical furniture.

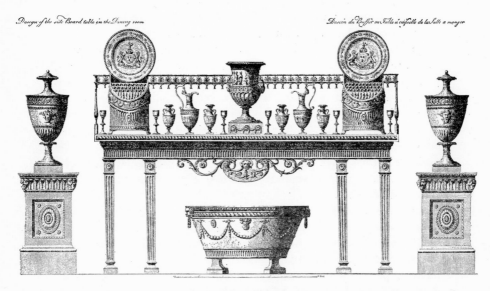

Figure a. 'Design of the side Board table in the Drawing room' at Kenwood, c. 1768–9. 'The Works in Architecture of Robert and James Adam,' Vol. 1, No. 2, Pl. viii (see fig. 19).

CHAPTER ONE

THE SOURCES OF THE ADAM STYLE

The Adam style may be appropriately described, in the words used by Sir Joshua Reynolds to define invention, as 'little more than a new combination of those images which have been previously gathered and deposited in the memory. . . .'[1]

Robert Adam was equipped with a vast store of 'images' gathered from a wide variety of sources, and an extraordinary ability to transform them into 'inventions' entirely new, and entirely his own. In fact, his synthesis of eclectic details is so complete that only a hint of the prototype lingers in the finished work. Yet, no matter how well his individual sources are disguised, the general influences of Scotland, Italy, and France are always discernible.

Since the Scottish and Italian contributions to his style have been fully presented by John Fleming and Sir John Summerson,[2] it will suffice here to briefly outline those elements which have some bearing upon furniture. Adam's relationship with France, on the other hand, is a much more complex, and relatively unexplored subject requiring a more detailed discussion.

Scotland. Robert Adam, born in Kirkcaldy, Fifeshire, on 3 July 1728, was the second of four sons of William Adam, the foremost Scottish architect of the time. His youth was spent in the stimulating atmosphere of his family's intellectual coterie, which included such notable figures as Adam Smith, David Hume, Adam Ferguson; the poets, William Wilkie, and Allan Ramsay; the historian, William Robertson; John MacGowan, a well-known collector of antiquities; Sir John Clerk of Penicuik, and others.

It was only at about the age of 18, after he had completed his formal education at Edinburgh High School, and University, that Robert decided upon an architectural career. Coupled with the practical training he received as apprentice to his father was the interest and respect for the best of English and Italian building which he gleaned from William Adam's cultured friends and patrons, especially Sir John Clerk of Penicuik. An architectural tour of England in 1749–50, and frequent perusal of the Neo-Palladian pattern books also contributed to the formation and refinement of his tastes. Thus, after William Adam's death in 1748, Robert was experienced enough to take over the practice with his elder brother John.

In the next five years he completed the work begun by his father at Fort George and Hopetoun, as well as his own designs for the building and decoration of Dumfries, his first entirely new project. These activities not only prepared him financially and professionally for the Grand Tour, but they also provided the three main interests that were to dominate the whole of his later work.

1. MOVEMENT—a quality epitomised by Vanbrugh, appreciated and adapted by William Adam, and inherent also in the 'staccato' of Kent's and Burlington's Palladianism. Movement is defined by Adam as 'the rise and fall, the advance and recess, with other diversity of form, in the different parts of a building, so as to add greatly to the picturesque of the composition. . . .'[3] What is expressed in Adam's words, and visible in his works is movement of a pictorial and surface character rather than the plastic qualities usually associated with the term.

2. SURFACE DECORATION—a taste largely acquired from his father's obvious dislike for the plain surface. Another omen of his interest in superficial variety may be found in his youthful attraction to the 'tinsel' Gothic and Chinese ornaments proffered by the pattern books of William Halfpenny, Batty Langley, and Robert Morris.

3. LIGHT AND ELEGANT INTERIOR DECORATION enters with the Rococo, a style which Adam employed in the plasterwork of Hopetoun (1752), and Dumfries (1754). In so far as it departs from the heavy architectural

interiors of Kent and the Neo-Palladians, the Rococo paves the way for Adam's gossamer decorations of the 1760s and 70s. His translation of antique motifs into effeminate embroideries is, in many respects, more characteristic of a Rococo point of view than a strictly classical one. Here the contrast between French and English Neo-classicism is extremely interesting. While the French revolted against the Rococo, taking the opposite and heavy forms of the *goût grec* or *style mâle,* the English, on the contrary, rejected the masculine heaviness of Palladianism in favour of lighter and more delicate forms. This is by no means to suggest that the Adam style of decoration is not classical. Although its linear expression, and lightness of form and colour are features common to the Rococo, its theory and content, and characteristic restraint are fully Neo-classical.

Italy. Leaving England in October 1754, Adam joined Charles Hope, brother of Lord Hopetoun, in Brussels and continued on through Belgium and France, across to Genoa, and down to Florence seeing things, laying in a stock of useful acquaintances for Rome and the future, and becoming more of a dandy as he went along. In Florence he had the great fortune to be introduced to the French architect and draughtsman, Charles-Louis Clérisseau, who agreed to accompany him to Rome as drawing master and guide. This was one of the most momentous occasions in Adam's career, for Clérisseau, having been a *Prix de Rome* student at the French Academy from 1749 to 1754, was not only familiar with the major monuments of Rome, but, more important, he had experienced the very first waves of Neo-classical thought and activity.

When Adam entered Rome in February 1755 the return to antiquity was well under way, and several painstaking investigations had already been completed. Among the earliest projects were Soufflot's drawings of the temples at Paestum in 1750; the surveys of Athens first by Stuart and Revett from 1751–5, and later in 1754–5 by Clérisseau's fellow architectural student, Julien David Le Roy (whose results appeared in print in 1758, four years before those of his English predecessors)[4]; and the work of Robert Wood and James Dawkins on the ruins of Palmyra and Balbec, published in 1753 and 1757 respectively. In a similar, but less architectural vein, Count Caylus had begun to issue his *Recueil d'Antiquités* in 1752; in 1754 Cochin published the *Observations sur les Antiquités de la Ville d'Herculanum* resulting from his revolutionary tour of antiquities made in 1749–51 with Soufflot, Le Blanc, and de Vandières, the future Marquis de Marigny; and Piranesi was publicizing his intense passion for Roman remains as subjects both of creative and of historical interest.[5]

Added to the achievements of the immediate past were the current activities of an impressive gathering of French and English *avant gardists* headquartering in Rome. Before long Adam, by his own initiative or Clérisseau's introduction, had made the acquaintance of the most important of these innovators, men like Piranesi, Winckelmann, and Robert Wood; the painters, Allan Ramsay, Gavin Hamilton, Raphael Mengs, Pompeo Batoni, and Laurent Pecheux who instructed him in drawing; the architects, Marie-Joseph Peyre, Moreau-Desproux, De Wailly, probably Le Roy, and many others. Stimulated by the accomplishments of his friends and predecessors, Adam approached the mecca of ancient civilization with unparalleled energy and enthusiasm. After three years of exchanging ideas, visiting ancient sites, studying, drawing, and collecting remains, the foundations of his style were well and truly laid. Its main components were as follows:

1. A collection of antique forms and ornaments large enough to sustain thirty years of Adam decoration. This was supplemented by the folio publications of Le Roy, and Stuart and Revett on Athens; Robert Wood on Balbec and Palmyra; the classical *pot pourris* of Montfaucon and Count Caylus; the coloured illustrations of William Hamilton's *Collection of Etruscan, Greek and Roman Antiquities* (Naples, 1766–67); the engravings of Santo Bartoli; and other works on Roman and especially Etruscan arts.

2. A well informed picture of the variety and what he called 'gaiety' of interior decoration and planning, derived from the Baths of Dio-

cletian and Caracalla, Hadrian's Villa at Tivoli, the remains at Baiae, and the new discoveries at Herculaneum and Pompeii.

3. Grotesque ornaments drawn from the Vatican Loggie, the Villa Madama, Caprarola, and other Renaissance interiors which he esteemed as accurate imitations of ancient domestic buildings known to the sixteenth century, but not to the eighteenth.

4. Experience in draughtsmanship and picturesque composition acquired under the guidance of Clérisseau and Laurent Pecheux. The importance which these two skills assumed in themselves, regardless of subject matter, is reflected in the graphic and decorative character of Adam's interpretation of antiquity.

5. Artistic licence sanctioned by the originality displayed by the ancients, and championed by Piranesi. Like all of his contemporaries, Adam fed upon antiquity as nourishment for his own creative genius.

6. An inordinate craving for success also partakes in the making of the Adam style. It drove him to amass the largest classical vocabulary, to be a superior draughtsman, to be continually and infinitely novel, and thus to eclipse his colleagues and overwhelm his patrons.

Figure b. Design of a table for the Vestibule at Syon, 1765. 'The Works in Architecture' Vol. III, Pl. xi (mislabelled for the Earl of Bute at Luton).

England. Adam returned to England in January 1758 bearing both the materials and the desire to create a new style—not so much of architecture as of decoration. As it happened, circumstance was entirely in his favour. A respect for the ancients ingrained by the long Palladian experience, a brief taste of the Rococo, a delight in eccentricity, which had admitted the Gothic and Chinese modes, and a growing preference for smaller houses with more intimate and varied rooms conspired to make the English fully receptive to his personal version of antiquity. Fortune also saw that the first demands made upon him were primarily for interior decoration, where he had the greatest opportunity to display his skills and vocabulary. His only disappointment was having to share the opening scene with his arch rival, James Stuart, who had not only outdone him in visiting Greece, but had also anticipated his Neo-classical style by a few years. Never- [1,2] theless, Stuart's precedence was more valuable than Adam would ever care to admit.

In 1759–60 Adam obtained his first great commission—the furnishing and decoration of Kedleston. This could hardly have pleased him more for, in addition to being a most desirable plum, it was a triumph [1] over Stuart who had already provided designs for decorating the house as early as 1757. To dress the interiors of Kedleston in an antique style was of course no problem for Adam. It was quite a different matter, however, to design furniture in the same mode. Here he had no practical experience, and few, if any models in antiquity. Fortunately, Kedleston was equipped both with Stuart's designs and with a professional cabinet-maker and furniture designer, John Linnell. Although Adam was quick to condemn Stuart's efforts in the most ridiculing terms,[6] he undoubtedly found them instructive. It can be no mere coincidence that his tripod candle-stand for Sir Nathaniel Curzon [1,2,3] (*c.* 1760–61) is almost identical to those in Stuart's designs for a Great Hall at Kedleston (*c.* 1757), and for the Painted Room at Spencer House, St. James's (1759), or that his sideboard follows the straight [4,5] Neo-classical lines of the tables in the two Stuart drawings. For seat furniture, on the other hand, there was no such convenient precedent.

8

Hence we find Adam resorting to the Kentian and Rococo forms provided by Linnell.

The next two or three years were a period of indecision during which he experimented with various compromises between the Kentian and classical styles. It was at this moment that he was brought into contact with French Neo-classicism.

Adam and France. When, in 1762, Adam embarked on his career as a furniture designer, Paris was already in the grips of the *goût grec*. The style had manifest itself in Lalive de Jully's furniture designed in 1756–7 by La Lorrain; in the numerous interiors illustrated in Neufforge's *Recueil d'Architecture* of which four volumes had appeared (1757, 1758, 1760, 1761) and five were yet to come (1763, 1765, 1767, 1768, and a Supplement of 30 *cahiers* published between 1772–7); in the table and chair accompanying the Marquis de Marigny in Roslin's portrait exhibited, complete with Neo-classical frame, at the *Salon* of 1761[7]; and no doubt in many other instances now unknown. By 1763 Grimm was able to report that '. . . *la mode en est devenue si générale que tout se fait aujord'hui à la grecque. La décoration extérieure et intérieure des batimens, les meubles, les étoffes, les bijoux de toute espèce, tout est à Paris à la grecque. . . .*'[8]

For Adam to have remained ignorant of such a rage for antiquity is unimaginable, especially since most of his patrons were avid followers of French fashion. He himself visited France only once in his lifetime —in 1754, and then, with the possible exception of a meeting with Cochin, found nothing particularly inspiring. Although he did witness the preparation of French Neo-classicism in Italy, it is unlikely that he encountered anything in the way of furniture at that date.

When he returned to England in 1758, communications with France were barred by the Seven Years War. Some of Neufforge's engravings may conceivably have reached him indirectly through Dutch or even Italian sources, but no positive link could be established until after the Treaty of 1763, when the 'milords' could once again partake of Parisian wares.

In August 1763, the sixth Earl of Coventry set off for Paris in search of tapestries, furniture, and glasses for the new Adam rooms at Croome Court.[9] He returned in the early Autumn bearing, amongst other things, designs for a Gobelins tapestry room. These were immediately delivered to Adam, who provided him in November with a 'Section of the Tapestry Room,' and in January 1764 with designs for 'Finishing the sides of the Tapestry Room,' and for 'Altering the French designs of the Tapestry Room in colours.'[10]

The tapestry in question was the very latest Gobelins invention with large medallions conceived in 1758 *'sur l'idée de M. Soufflot'*[11] to contain pictures by Boucher. In order to prevail upon and *'faire décider'* prospective customers, a *tableau* had been prepared in 1762 *'répresentant un Apartement tel qu'il doit être, avec les tentures de la tapisserie, le lit, le fauteuil et le canapé.'*[12] As the Gobelins was extremely anxious to sell the whole of its package deal, there can be no doubt that the design presented to Lord Coventry was a copy of the prospectus including the furniture.

Lord Coventry was the first of five customers, four of them patrons of Robert Adam, to purchase the tapestry as well as the matching upholstery.[13] Oddly enough, each of the four Englishmen, although employing a different cabinet-maker, obtained a suite of chairs and sofas with straight legs and oval backs, the latter to accord with the medallion theme. The similarity of these suites pre-supposes a common source—Adam or the Gobelins.

Credit is traditionally given to Robert Adam who thus, according to the late Fiske Kimball, would have anticipated and influenced the genesis of the Louis XVI style.[14] Yet, not a single Adam design for these pieces exists, nor are any recorded in the surviving accounts of his work at Croome Court and Moor Park, wherein every other design, no matter how small or rough, is billed and described.[15] The basic pattern, if not the actual design, for the tapestry suites must therefore have originated from the *Manufacture du Roi,* and possibly from Soufflot who had already provided furniture in the 'antique' style in 1763 for the Marquis de Marigny.[16]

120

At this critical moment in Adam's career, the appearance of French designs was surely of some interest and assistance. Their immediate **104** influence may be seen in the window stool executed *c.* 1765 for the Gallery at Croome Court. This stool, originally proposed in 1764 for the Saloon at Moor Park,[17] is, as far as we know, England's first fully Neo-classical piece of seat furniture. By no mere chance, its design coincides with Sir Laurence Dundas's plans for transforming the Gallery at Moor Park into a tapestry room like that which Adam had just experienced at Croome Court. For some reason the stool was rejected by Dundas, and in February 1765 was presented and billed to Lord Coventry for whom it was executed. The surviving drawing, because it is inscribed for Dundas, has been mistakenly identified with **105** the *'banquette'* belonging to the Moor Park tapestry suite—an understandable error indeed. Although the two pieces may ultimately derive from a common French source, they are, however, far too different in composition and detail to have been made from the same design.

Fortunately, we do have one fully documented example of Adam's use of French material. Among his bills to Lord Coventry is one dated 6 May 1767 for 'A Tripod altered from a French design for a Water **134** Stand.'[18] This bill corresponds with a rapid pencil sketch in the Soane Museum, inscribed 'Lord Coventry's tripod(?) for,' with the words 'Water Stand' boldly written over. Out of the rough drawing with its *pentimenti* came the two tripod candle-stands published in the first **135,136** volume of Adam's *Works,* one of which was executed for both Sir Laurence Dundas and the Duke of Bolton. Although Lord Coventry's French design provided Adam with the idea and opportunity of translating a classical form into furniture, the form itself was no revelation. The tripod was a well known type of Roman sacrificial altar, which had already been employed as a small candle-stand, first by James **1,2,3,6,** Stuart in his designs for Kedleston (*c.* 1757) and Spencer House (1759),[19] **152** and shortly afterwards (before 1761) by Adam. Like most of the components of Adam's classical vocabulary, it had also been reduced to a two-dimensional ornament, and used, for example, in the stucco decorations of the Long Gallery at Syon *c.* 1763–4. Presumably the tripod had made its first appearance as a proper article of furniture in France, just before Adam's sketch of 1767; however, no executed examples of that early date survive.

Adam's experience of French classicism was neither limited to furniture, nor to the acquisitions of Lord Coventry and the other Gobelins patrons. In 1766 he designed a 'French' room for Miss Anne Pitt at Kensington Gore, using a rather ordinary ceiling design which had assumed special value being the work of a French draughtsman, commissioned by the well known Mariette, and acquired and approved by Horace Walpole.[20] As executor of Miss Pitt's French commissions, Adam must also have seen her designs for commodes which Walpole had obtained from Simon-Philippe Poirier, one of the leading Parisian *marchand—merciers*.[21] While we know nothing at all about these commodes, it is quite possible that they were to be ornamented with the Sèvres plaques for which Poirier was famous. This kind of ornamentation, whether it was seen on Anne Pitt's designs, or on other French pieces, bears comparison with Adam's later use of inset paintings on all types of furniture.

26,70, *etc.*

From 1765 onwards a steadily increasing amount of Louis XVI furniture crossed the Channel, much of it destined for the town and country houses in which Adam was employed. Here was a continuous source of up-to-date information on the very latest Parisian modes. Its influence can be seen in Adam's gilt brass, and ormolu mounts, his ever present festoons, his soaring pier glasses, and more specifically in such pieces as the gold and white bookcase designed for Sir George Colebrooke in 1771, the *turquoise* of the early 1770s also for Colebrooke, and the *confident* for Sir Abraham Hume, 1780.

42
113,124

In addition to the designs and pieces in the possession of his patrons, there was a wealth of material readily available in J.-F. Neufforge's *Recueil,* the earliest collection of exclusively Neo-classical designs for buildings, interiors, furniture, decorative objects, and iron work. We know from the sale of Adam's library[22] that he did in fact possess at least the 4th (1761), 5th (1763), and 6th (1765) volumes of this extremely important work. Although the ponderous severity of Neufforge's classicism, and for that matter of the *goût grec* in general, is inimical to Adam's taste for gaiety and movement, it was nevertheless useful and informative, especially in the early stages of his career. What seems to have interested him most in Neufforge was : 1) Designs for iron balustrades which became the models for the typical and much admired Adam stair rails (Vol. V, pl. 310); 2) a table supported on scrolled brackets ending in straight tapered legs which anticipate

b the forms of a table designed in 1765 for the Vestibule at Syon (Vol. V, pl. 297); 3) the medallions ornamenting virtually every Neufforge design—a favourite Adam motif which first appears in the projects

98 for the Kedleston sofa, 1762 and earlier; 4) the combination of a tall

57, *etc.* mirror and a table or commode, forming an entire wall decoration—a common French practice which Adam continued to develop.

It is not to be imagined, however, that the traffic in classical notions moved in only one direction. The publication of Adam's *Works* with a text in French as well as English, contributed enormously to the international influence of his style. Anglo mania, which introduced such Adam inventions as the lyre back chair and the Etruscan style, was as rampant in Paris as Gallo mania was in London. The frantic interchange of fashionable antiques is epitomized in an amusing anecdote related by Josiah Wedgwood in 1768. 'Mr. Boulton tells me I shod be surprised to know what a trade has lately been made out of Vases at Paris. The Artists have even come over to London, picked up all the old whimsical ugly things they could meet with, carried them to Paris where they have mounted & ornamented them with metal, & sold them to the Virtuosi of every Nation, & particularly to Millords d'Anglise, for the greatest raritys. . . .'[23]

Figure c. '*Girandole in the first Drawing room*' at *Derby House, Grosvenor Square, 1774.* '*The Works in Architecture*' *Vol. II, No. 1, Pl. vii (see fig. 93).*

CHAPTER TWO

THE DEVELOPMENT OF ADAM FURNITURE

In the popular image Adam furniture virtually begins and ends with his mature style. This fragmentary picture has become so universally accepted that there is no longer any concept of stylistic development. Yet, within the span of his career it is possible to distinguish four different periods : 1. EARLY 1762–1764; 2. TRANSITIONAL 1765–1768; 3. MATURE 1769–1777; 4.LATE 1778–1792. As certain forms develop faster than others, none of these periods is without some irregularities. Furthermore, one must expect not only the normal measure of exceptions, overlappings, and repetitions found in the work of any artist, but also those dictated by the length of time involved in furnishing, and by the personal tastes and requirements of the client.

The early style 1762–1764. The first three years of Adam's career as a furniture designer were spent in search of an appropriate Neo-classical style. He began in 1762 with no experience in the field, no preconceived ideas of what 'antique' furniture should be, no models in antiquity, and as yet little knowledge of the *goût grec*. All that he had to guide him was a few designs by James Stuart. Following Stuart's direction, he immediately arrived at the Kedleston sideboard. From this remarkably classical composition one would automatically expect his succeeding designs to be variations and improvements upon the initial pattern of straight legs and simple forms. Had such been the case his mature style would probably have been apparent by the mid 1760s, and the furniture at Moor Park or Syon might then have resembled that at Osterley. But this, as we know, was not the case. Instead he chose to experiment with the combination of antique orna-

1,2

3–5

ments and restrained Rococo or Kentian forms. Obviously he could 8,102,103 not have been entirely convinced that the Kedleston sideboard was the only answer, or even the right one. The cause of his doubts is indeed puzzling. It may well be that such regular shapes seemed at first too restrictive for his vast decorative vocabulary, and too rigid for his taste for movement. In any event, he must certainly have hoped that his alternative path would ultimately lead him to a more satisfactory, and perhaps more original solution.

At this early stage cabriole legs, squarish architectural case furniture, and bulky mirror frames are the main recipients of his sphinxes, grif- 37,52,102, etc. fons, rams' heads, urns, acanthus, and other classical motifs. These ornaments are conventionally arranged either in well defined compartments, in distinct groups, or at regular intervals, following, in each instance, the structural divisions of the piece. Accents fall abruptly on terminal elements—rams' head or term capitals, paw feet, and acanthus crests—which are augmented in size, and rendered in high relief and naturalistic detail. The result is a slow moving 'staccato' of separate parts, a familiar Neo-Palladian mannerism, which is also present in early Adam interior and exterior designs. Needless to say, such compromises could neither be termed 'antique,' nor revolutionary.

Not until after his experience of French Neo-classical designs in 1764–5 did Adam begin to return to the style of the Kedleston sideboard. What happens after this is markedly different from anything that had previously occurred in England.

The transitional style 1765–1768. The furniture of the late 1760s embodies all the seeds of the mature Adam style, but lacks its exaggerated delicacy, its fluency, and sophisticated polish. As a result it is, in many respects and to many tastes, the most palatable and interesting of Adam's inventions. There are no extremes, no general formulae, and no overall schemes of decoration into which everything is submerged. The transitional phase finds Adam sampling, selecting, and gradually refining.

Straight legs rapidly become legion. At first they maintain a block-ish architectural outline which lends an air of solidity to the piece as a whole. The progress from this to the more slender tapered leg of the 1770s epitomizes the making of the Adam style. Meanwhile, for a brief period *c*. 1767–8, he experiments with a complicated type of baluster leg worked into lotus forms, enriched with multiple capitals, and terminated by ornamented ball feet. Such diversity undoubtedly appealed to his interest in movement, but that appeal was only moment-ary. Having been employed on the Osterley sideboard, on several tables for Lansdowne House, and for the Earl of Coventry's in Picca-dilly, the form was soon dropped in favour of the more restrained types of straight legs.

Case furniture of this period is always rectangular. The semi-circular shape, although used for tables, is not applied to commodes until the 1770s. Decoration is still confined to recessed panels, and to the frieze, mouldings, and other structural divisions. Classicizing is thus more a matter of disciplined composition than of new forms such as were required for chairs and tables.

Mirrors develop rather slowly, but later accelerate into the most advanced representatives of the Adam style. The tidying-up process does not begin until about 1767 when elaborate side and corner orna-ments are drawn in, and concentrated on the frame itself. As a result, the entire piece emerges with a much more regular outline, and restrained appearance. Traditional mitred-corner frames with profile terms, and husk festoons at the sides are an exception occurring several times in the 1760s, but rarely afterwards.

Unlike the *goût grec,* Adam's interpretation of antiquity depends less upon form than upon ornament. In the latter he is better versed, freer, and more confident, and therefore matures with much greater speed and consistency. By 1768 the major part of his enormous decorative vocabulary is in view. Greek frets, Vitruvian scrolls, and various an-themion and guilloche patterns are his main repetitive ornaments. Individual motifs include sphinxes, griffons, term figures, rams' heads, human and animal masks, putti, medallions, urns, candelabra, tripods, anthemion, acanthus, husk festoons, rosettes, and patera. Architectural elements—friezes, cornices, capitals, pilasters, and the like—also serve as enrichments.

This vocabulary is not peculiar to Adam alone, but was the common property of every artist who had visited Rome, or was familiar with the volumes of Montfaucon, Count Caylus, and others. Although several classical motifs had already appeared in Kentian furniture, and in French pieces of the late 1750s and early 60s, no other designer had ever employed so many of them with such constancy and originality. Yet, it is not the number, but the handling of these ornaments that characterizes the Adam style.

Motifs chosen for their antique pedigree are freely dissected, combined, reduced in size, and refined. The aim is, in Adam's own words, 'to transfuse the beautiful spirit of antiquity with novelty and variety'[24]; the result—a limitless array of motifs often more Adam than antique. Their application to furniture is somewhat self conscious, and not always integrated. They are closely grouped at regular intervals, much as they were in the earlier period, but are rendered in lower relief. What is notably lacking is the selectivity and spatial adjustments that make Adam's later decoration so fluid and elegant.

Antique forms are not only employed as ornaments, but also as structural members, accessories, and even as entire pieces of furniture. A lyre, as Horace Walpole wittily observed, 'make(s) a charming harmony'[25] as the back of a chair. While sacrificial altars become perfume burners or candle-stands, urns and pedestals are transformed into wine coolers and cellarettes. Using a sideboard as a kind of stage, Adam arranges these useful and decorative objects into a kind of picturesque display. The sideboard composition, first introduced at Kedleston in 1762, becomes a typical Adam theme intended more as wall decoration than as an independent piece of furniture.

The furniture of this period is either entirely gilded, or is painted white with gilt details. Other colours are not yet employed except in decorative medallions which first appear in 1768. Natural wood, usually mahogany, is common for seat furniture, but is otherwise

(margin notes: 106; 6,132–140, etc.; a,3)

exceptional, and in the following decade disappears almost entirely. In the execution of ornaments, carved wood is gradually replaced by metal and composition.[26] The main attraction of such synthetic materials was their combination of strength, lightness, and malleability. Unlike wood, they could be shaped into extremely intricate and delicate forms which, requiring little support from the structure, could be applied almost anywhere. The result is to be seen mainly in the increasing occurrence, and delicacy, of pendant and tracery motifs. Nevertheless, as much as these materials facilitated the Adam style, they did not determine it.

What we are able to distinguish as an intermediate stage in Adam's style was, to his contemporaries, a final statement which they undoubtedly found appealing enough to imitate immediately. In fact, the substantial character of the work of this period seems to have met with more approval than the over refined pieces which followed.

The mature style 1769–1777. By 1773 Adam could justly boast of having revolutionized English interior design. Armed with a stylish, albeit corrupt translation of antiquity, he became the unchallenged arbiter of taste. He met the increased demands for his services rapidly and effortlessly, with a stream of variations upon a few themes. His furniture, instead of being tentative and uneven, is now remarkably fluent and homogeneous. Regardless of what or where it is, every piece is smooth, subtle, slight, and streamlined.

Wall furniture (mirrors, girandoles, tables, and commodes), and decorative pieces (urns, pedestals, and tripods) dominate his *oeuvre*.
44–47 Semi-circular commodes replace the more masculine rectangular ones.
21–25, *etc.* Tables are pared down to a narrow frieze and slender tapered legs. The arrangement of the legs in pairs separated by a wide central
24 interval is one of Adam's typical methods of spacing elements and dividing areas. This device not only provides more movement and variety, but it also tends to emphasize the delicacy of the parts as well as the whole.

Girandoles, previously formed of glass framed by lively acanthus scrolls, are now highly restrained compositions of medallions, urns, tripods, sphinxes, and other motifs delicately balanced one above the other. **c,d 92–95**

Mirrors reveal Adam at his best. Tall pier glasses are reduced to a chaste and almost sleek pattern of a narrow flat frame surmounted by a crest. Given a larger wall space, however, he introduces an entirely new and different form—a tripartite mirror divided by female terms or filigree pilasters laid on to the glass. The raised centre, of square or arched shape, ornamented with fanlight tracery patterns, conveys the impression of a Palladian window. Friezes and railings further underline the architectural illusion. Here the frame is deprived of its normal function as a confining border, and the glass becomes a field for ornament. This type of mirror is one of Adam's most original inventions, and is also the epitome of his attitude towards furniture. **69–71**, *etc.* **62,63** **66–67, 72–73**, *etc.*

No Adam house is complete without a pair of urns and pedestals, and at least one tripod. The genesis of the latter begins, as already noted, in 1767 with a French design in the possession of the Earl of Coventry. The basic formula of a bowl supported on tall slender legs gives way to innumerable variations, among them a special type with enclosed sides and pierced ornaments. **134** **135–143**

The range of seat furniture is enlarged to include sofas, *confidents,* arm chairs, hall chairs, and stools. Like everything else, each piece is subjected to the endless process of reduction and refinement. The results are much less rigid, more graceful and delicate than his earlier efforts. Shapes are essentially simple, curved or angular, relying mainly upon ornament for variation. **66,113-124**

In the whole of his career Adam designed, as far as we know, only seven beds.[27] Almost all of them are conceived as miniature garden temples with domed canopies supported on columnar posts. **125–129**

The furniture of this period is neither assertive nor autonomous. Each piece has but a minimal effect in its own right, for not only is it designed for a particular room, and usually for a particular situation (a niche, a pier, etc.) as well, but it is normally painted and ornamented **35,129, 145**, *etc.*

to match the surrounding decorations, and may also be joined to another piece to form a single unit. A mirror, for example, instead of being an independent object, is brought down to meet the edge of a table or commode of identical width. The vertical divisions of the glass are continued in the legs or compartments of the piece below. In addition, the base of the mirror is frequently overlaid with an ornamental urn or gallery, which appears to belong to the table. Hence, it is not always easy, especially on paper, to tell where one piece begins and the other ends.

51,62,74,
etc.

57,62,79,
etc.

Taken out of its original context, Adam furniture is often quite difficult to distinguish from the designs of his contemporaries, and even from later imitations. Although there is no clear cut rule by which to identify a *bona fide* Adam piece, the interpretation and use of ornament is usually the best criterion.

After constant refinements, his classical vocabulary is finally transformed into a standard code of brief, linear forms. These are arranged according to a few carefully devised formulae, which are repeated over and over again. By simply adding or subtracting motifs, substituting different ones, and rearranging the order, he emerges with an infinite number of different compositions. However intricate his patterns may be, they are seldom fussy for he is always restrained and selective. Units tend to be openly spaced in a way that emphasizes their miniscule size and delicacy. They are frequently supported and strung together on fragile chains of husks or bell flowers, a device which lends itself well to a fully ornamented surface. Medallions and tablets containing figures of classical derivation serve as focal points. These forms may be found perched on pedestals, worked into grotesques, superimposed over smaller and contrasting shapes (usually a simple bar or low platform), and in several other combinations. They are also introduced as actual plaques tacked on to a frieze or frame to add movement, depth, and variety.

44,64,69,
etc.

26,29,33,
etc.

Adam's linear patterns are used not only for enrichment but also for articulation. Semi-circular commodes, for instance, are first divided in three by slight pilasters. The decoration of the central panel is then

44,45,47

arranged in groups or compartments repeating the larger tripartite division. (It is worth noting that this kind of division was extremely common on French commodes of the period, which must have been known to Adam.) Likewise, tripartite mirrors are subdivided by horizontal bands or friezes on which additional motifs are supported and suspended. These highly controlled decorations cover and partition the piece without disturbing its flat surface.

63,66–67, 73, *etc.*

As a rule, furniture is either gilded, or painted, with soft pastel colours preferred to the hardness of white. Marquetry, although frequently used by professional cabinet-makers, is extremely rare in Adam's work. Instead, ornaments are either painted directly on to the coloured or gilded ground, or are executed in metal or composition, and overlaid. These synthetic materials are admirably suited to Adam's all-over decoration for they permit a more rapid, inexpensive, and uniform execution than would be possible with carving or inlay. Their widespread use in his interiors approaches a form of mass production, wherein the hand of the craftsman is barely perceptible.

117

67

Colour plays a major role in Adam's mature work. While flat tones define and intensify motifs, repeated colours unite them. What little accent there is, is provided by darker or brighter units. Colour is also used to imitate other materials, especially Wedgwood ceramics, and to denote particular styles. Etruscan furniture depends not upon ornament or shape, but upon the contrast of either black, terracotta, and white imitating Etruscan (or more correctly Greek) vases, or blue, brown, and white, a lighter combination, probably inspired by classical cameos, and infinitely better suited for interior decoration. This style, invented by Adam *c.* 1772–3, was employed in designs for Derby House, Osterley, Home House, Apsley House, George Keate's in Charlotte Street, Newby, Cumberland House, and Byram. The antique in its more splendid sense is generally represented by jewel-like reds, blues, and greens mated with gilt.

34,116–7, 127,145, *etc.*

66,67

Colour is above all the most immediate means of relating individual pieces to each other, and to the whole room. Not only do the walls, ceilings, and various furnishings share the same motifs, colours, and materials, but in several cases they are also executed by the same hand.

The late style 1778–1792. The last phase in Adam's career, from the late 1770s until his death in 1792, witnesses a decline in both the quantity and quality of his furniture. This has several explanations. When he began designing Neo-classical furniture the field was almost entirely his own. By 1775, however, his competitors were legion. Most of them, notably James Wyatt, James Paine, George Richardson, Thomas Leverton, Chippendale, and Linnell, were equally prolific and adept at translating antiquity into decoration, a practice which by then was international. Even more dampening was the American Revolution which so dented finances that little money was available for the pretty extravagances in which Adam excelled. The debility of his work may also be credited to his own basic procedure. Everything is further refined, simplified, and standardized. He is increasingly reliant upon cast and painted decoration. In short, the spirit of invention fades away into smoothness, and bland sophistication.

33,51,74, 143, *etc.*

Girandole in
the Nich of the
Etruscan room

Girandole dans la
Niche de la
Chambre Étrusque

Figure d. 'Girandole in the Nich of the Etruscan room" at Derby
House, Grosvenor Square, c. 1774. 'The Works in Architecture'
Vol. II, No. 1, Pl. viii (see fig. 93).

CHAPTER THREE

FURNISHING AND FURNITURE MAKING

The furnishing of Adam interiors. The extraordinary range of Adam's inventions, including everything from beds to ink-wells, is a constant and valid source of amazement. Unfortunately, it is also cause for exaggerating his responsibilities at the expense of many first rate cabinet-makers. Illusions of his complete and meticulous control over the furnishing of each interior are dispelled by an examination of the corpus of drawings in the Soane Museum. The number of houses for which he supplied anything approaching a complete range of furniture is exceedingly small—Osterley, Derby House (demolished 1862), and possibly Sir Abraham Hume's in Hill Street. For the vast majority, he provided either no furniture whatsoever, or a limited number of pieces, which, like mirrors, could be considered wall decorations. How then were Adam rooms furnished?

Unlike building, furnishing need not be a highly organized and harmonious procedure. It was as much, if not more, a matter of satisfying personal tastes and desires as of fulfilling necessities. The client, normally restricted to one architect at a time, was free to patronize any number of cabinet-makers simultaneously,[28] and to acquire pieces in any variety of styles, no matter how discordant with each other or with the decoration of the room. Those gentlemen who had employed Adam as the most fashionable architect were more than likely to seek out the most fashionable cabinet-makers as well. In fact, almost all of Adam's major interiors are associated with the most distinguished names in the world of English furniture. Ince and Mayhew supplied pieces to Croome Court, Lansdowne House, and 20 St. James's Square; William France worked at Kenwood; John Linnell is recorded at Kedleston,

Shardeloes, Mrs. Montagu's house in Hill Street, and Osterley; and Chippendale was employed at David Garrick's houses in the Adelphi and at Hampton, at Harewood, Kimbolton Castle, Nostell Priory, Mersham le Hatch, Lansdowne House, Alnwick, Saltram, and at Kenwood, where he acted not as a furniture maker, but as a mirror purveyor.

For the *beau monde,* visiting cabinet-makers and other craftsmen was both a social pastime and a practical way of obtaining the latest in furnishings. Lady Shelburne's diary provides a vivid account of a shopping tour made in 1768, at the very moment that Adam was decorating Lansdowne House:

> Saturday . . . . we first went to Zucchi's where we saw some ornaments for our ceilings, and a large architecture painting for the antichamber, with which however my Lord is not particularly pleased. From there to Mayhew and Inch [*sic*] where is some beautiful cabinet work, and two pretty cases for one of the rooms in my apartment, and which, though they are only deal, and to be painted white, he charges £50 for. From thence to Cipriani's where we saw some beautiful drawings and where Lord Shelburne bespoke some to be copied for me, to compleat my dressing room, which I wish should be finished with drawings, and crayon pictures. From thence to Zuccarelli's where we also saw some pictures doing for us and from thence home it being half an hour past four.[29]

Thomas Giffard of Chillington Park, Staffordshire, was making the rounds almost a year before he employed Adam. On 7 September 1771 he called on Josiah Wedgwood and told him '. . . he was going to build & shd be a good customer for Bass reliefs both as furniture & to set in stucco.'[30] Unfortunately, Giffard's initiative came to nought for, although he received designs from Adam in 1772, he died in 1776 before anything was completed.

The acme of fashion was to do one's buying in Paris. Horace Walpole's Parisian journals record almost daily visits to the *marchands-merciers,* often to execute commissions for his friends at home. Adam patrons—the Earl of Coventry, William Weddell, Sir Laurence Dundas, Sir Henry Bridgeman, the Earl of March, and others—are among the countless Englishmen who imported French pieces and designs in the latest *style antique*.

With so many cabinet-makers available at home and abroad, it seems difficult to imagine why Adam was called upon at all. The explanation lies partly in his patron's desire, perhaps at his suggestion, to have at least a few objects *en suite* with the new antique decorations. Normally, stylistic continuity only embraced mirrors, side tables, or other pieces constituting a wall composition, and possibly some accessories, like tripods, urns, and pedestals. For pieces so intimately related to his decorative schemes, Adam was the obvious and, at first, the only choice. But his style caught on with amazing speed, and it was not long before more alert craftsmen like John Linnell and Thomas Chippendale were able to match his interiors with furniture of their own design.

Adam and Chippendale. Chippendale's astonishing mastery of the Adam style, and frequent employment in Adam houses are traditionally interpreted as evidence not of his great skill and reputation, but of a partnership, wherein Adam provided designs and Chippendale executed them. This happy alliance has been convincingly exploded as a myth by the late R. W. Symonds.[31] While there is no doubt that Chippendale was influenced by Adam, there is also, as Mr. Symonds has demonstrated, no reason for presuming that he ever required or received any assistance from him. In fact, what evidence there is points to the contrary.

The splendid Neo-classical furniture at Harewood is commonly upheld as the epitome of the Adam-Chippendale union. Yet, there are no designs or bills from Adam, as there are from Chippendale,[32] to associate him with any part of the furnishing of the house. His authorship can also be ruled out on stylistic grounds. The choice and hand- 9,151 ling of ornament, the shape of the parts, and the general proportioning of the major Harewood pieces are typical of Chippendale, but markedly different from any authenticated Adam design. One must therefore eliminate Adam at Harewood, giving Chippendale his due credit.

Nostell Priory presents a more complex situation for there Adam and Chippendale were both supplying furniture, each to his own design. Among the many pieces known to have come from Chippendale is a set of six lyre back arm chairs executed in 1768, at least a **107** year after those designed by Adam for Osterley. A comparison of the **106** two chairs leaves no doubt that the Nostell set was made and designed by Chippendale. Not only does his adaptation of the lyre splat lack the delicacy of Adam's invention, but his use of an ornamented seat rail, and turned, fluted, and carved legs, while displaying his skill as a carver, destroys the elegance of design and proportion expressed in Adam's simple fluted frame. That Sir Rowland Winn was content with an imitation by Chippendale, when he could easily have obtained designs from Adam, seems very strange indeed. Evidently the chairs, being free standing furniture, belonged exclusively to Chippendale's commission, and were thus off-limits to Adam. On the other hand, the side tables for the Hall and Salon must have been considered close **28–30** enough to wall decoration to be included in the duties of the interior decorator. For these pieces, Adam provided the design as well as the craftsman, and Chippendale had no part whatsoever.

An even sharper division of labour is encountered at Mersham le Hatch, Adam's only complete country house, all of his others being older buildings to which he made additions and improvements. Mersham, having been wholly built and decorated by Adam, was turned over to Chippendale for furnishing. Although at this point Adam's employment formally terminated, he apparently continued to supply advice. On the 17 November 1774, Lady Grace Knatchbull wrote to inform him that she was '. . . in town for one day & wished to have half an hour conference . . . . concerning the furniture for her drawing room.'[33] While it is altogether possible that she received rough sketches as well as verbal comments from Adam, her designs invariably came from Chippendale. This is confirmed by a letter from the latter to Sir Edward Knatchbull, 23 June 1778, notifying him that he had sent designs for pier glasses, girandoles, and '. . . an Axminster Carpet to Correspond with your Ceiling to go into the Bow.'[34] The ceiling was of course Adam's, as was the idea of matching carpets. Nevertheless, the designs for the carpet, and for the other pieces on which Adam was consulted were not his responsibility, but Chippendale's.

Mersham, Nostell, and Harewood are ample testimony of Chippendale's ability and willingness to design furniture in the Adam style without Adam's assistance. According to Mr. Symonds,[35] this absence of collaboration was partly the result of Adam's lack of confidence in Chippendale's sometimes dilatory procedure. There is, however, no evidence for any such animosity. As each man was a skilled and fashionable specialist in a different field, the patron was more than likely, and certainly free to employ both at the same time for entirely different purposes. Although Adam was often called upon to provide advice and designs for furniture, he was never mistaken for a professional cabinet-maker.

The foregoing discussions have touched upon the large amounts of furniture not designed by Adam. It now remains to investigate the execution of those pieces which he did design.

The execution of Adam furniture. Adam's designs, having been approved, were either returned to him to be executed according to his direction, or were passed on by the client to the cabinet-maker entrusted with the furnishing of the house. In putting the designs entirely in the hands of first rate craftsmen, and thus ensuring superior quality, the latter procedure was the more advantageous. But the craftsmen concerned were employed not only to make furniture, but also to design it. Consequently, in the early stages, one finds men like John Linnell at Kedleston and Shardeloes, or William France at Kenwood producing their own Rococo inventions alongside Adam's Neo-classical ones. The extreme paradox occurs in the Kenwood Library when an Adam sofa is (or was)[36] *en suite* with a set of cabriole chairs by William France. This situation, in spite of its discordant results, was highly beneficial both to Adam and to the cabinet-maker. For one it provided experienced hints in the practical requirements of furniture design, and for the other an introduction to the new style. The course of this

exchange can be followed in detail in the various projects by **Adam** 97–98,101
and Linnell for the Kedleston sofa.

In the method of contracting described above, the key figure was
the cabinet-maker. Adam's participation was limited to supplying the
designs and directing the placement of the finished pieces in the room.
When, on the other hand, the execution of his designs was included in
his commission as architect and decorator, Adam was responsible not
only for choosing the maker, but also for supervising the work, and
approving, and often paying the accounts.

As a rule, the craftsmen he selected were already in his employ in
capacities other than furniture making. Thus, as carver for Lansdowne
House, John Gilbert was called upon to supply mirrors, tables, chimney   **18**
pieces, doors, mouldings, and even 'fig leaves to figures in ye niches.'[37]
Similarly, Richard Collins, carpenter and Clerk of Works at 20 St.
James's Square, was responsible for making Adam's bookcase for **Lady**   **48**
Williams Wynne. The piece was then ornamented by Antonio Zucchi,
whose main task was to provide paintings for the walls and ceilings of
the house. Needless to say, this communal system held no attraction
for expert cabinet-makers with flourishing practices of their own.
Fortunately, however, Adam's later designs, depending largely upon
painted and moulded ornaments, did not require the skills of highly
specialized craftsmen like Linnell, France, or Chippendale. Whatever
may have been lost in quality as a result of this procedure was made
up in continuity of workmanship as well as design.

CHAPTER FOUR

THE REPUTATION OF THE ADAM STYLE

EIGHTEENTH CENTURY TO TWENTIETH CENTURY

For the last three decades of the eighteenth century the Adam style was esteemed the zenith of fashion. So unanimous was its acceptance that it became a truly national idiom affecting the work of virtually every English cabinet-maker and designer—Matthias Lock, John Linnell, Matthew Darly, Thomas Chippendale junior and senior, Ince and Mayhew, Hepplewhite, Sheraton, Pergolesi, John Carter, George Richardson, James Wyatt, James Paine, and Henry Keene being but a prominent selection.

9,107-109, 146–147, 151,154

What the public adored was not so much the antique provenance of the style as its feminine lightness and gaiety. Yet, these were also the qualities for which Adam was criticized. From Sir William Chambers, the protagonist of eclectic Palladianism, came the terse and expected comment, 'filigrane toy work.'[38] Horace Walpole, as usual, had much more to say. 'Gingerbread and sippets of embroidery,'[39] 'filigraine and fan painting,'[40] 'shreds, remnants, and *clinquant*'[41] are only a few of his many mocking epithets all of which are as appropriate to his own Strawberry Hill Gothic as to Adam's antiquities. However inconsistent Walpole's tastes may be, his statement of regret that 'From Kent's mahogany we are dwindled to Adam's filigree. Grandeur and simplicity are not yet a fashion'[42] is nevertheless the most poignant expression of the conservative attitudes of this period.

To the following generation, caught up in the Greek revival and in serious archeological studies, the Adam style was not only too 'trivial' and 'tawdry,' but, even worse it was a corruption of already debased forms of antiquity. Although the character of Adam's work was thus discredited, the importance of his revolution in interior design was not forgotten, nor was his great gift for invention. Of all the early nineteenth century criticisms, the most equitable was that presented by Sir John Soane in his Royal Academy Lectures :

> . . . it is to the activity of the Messrs. Adam that we are more particularly indebted for breaking the talismanic charm, which the fashion of the day had imposed, and for the introduction from Ancient Works of a light and fanciful style of Decoration . . . The Messrs. Adam had not formed their Taste on the best examples of Antiquity, and therefore using the same style in Public and Private Buildings, internally and externally, they did not retain the favourable opinion of the Public to the extent expected . . . However Mr. Adam may occasionally, in his flights of fancy have descended to trifles, and given an elegance and an importance to a Sedan Chair, or to the Keyhole of a Lady's Escritoire, let us, in candour and justice to departed merit, remember that in the preceding age, the great . . . Kent . . . was likewise consulted for designs for State Coaches, City Barges and Children's Cradles.[43]

Similar objections to Adam's sources were voiced in less benevolent terms by Charles Tatham,[44] and even by the great Adam imitator, James Wyatt.[45]

The conservative reaction reached its extreme in the devastating attack levelled by Joseph Gwilt in his *Encyclopedia of Architecture,* 1842. Here James Stuart, the paragon of 'chasteness and purity,' is pitted against

> . . . the opposite and vile taste of Robert Adam, a fashionable architect whose eye had been ruined by the corruptions of the worst period in Roman art. It can scarcely be believed, the ornaments of Diocletian's palace at Spalatro should have loaded our dwellings contemporaneously with the use among the more refined few of the exquisite exemplars of Greece, and even of Rome, in its better days. Yet such is the fact; the depraved compositions of Adam were not only tolerated but had their admirers. It is not to be supposed that the works of a man who was content to draw his supplies from so vitiated a source will require a lengthened notice.[46]

If the account in Gwilt's *Encyclopedia* is the most caustic of the century, that in Robert Stuart's *Dictionary of Architecture c.* 1830 is at once the most laudatory and rational.

> His style . . . ought not, in fairness, to be subjected to a scrutiny or comparison with that founded on the imitation of Greek buildings, of which little or nothing was then known, but with that of his contemporaries and his models. It will then be found abounding in beauties of a high and original kind, and which, it is hoped, will long preserve them as examples of a style of arrangement and decoration to which we would give our unqualified admiration, had they been the production of an architect of the lower Roman empire.[47]

While the extreme views of Gwilt and Stuart remained fairly isolated, the Soanian mean became the pattern for early and mid-Victorian critics, men like W. H. Leeds, James Fergusson, and T. L. Donaldson. Leeds, crediting Adam's 'great improvements in domestic architecture,' spurns his furniture for abandoning 'one faulty extreme (the Neo-Palladian) for another by pushing lightness to fragility and indulging in a profusion of ornament intended to combine delicacy with richness but partaking of flippery and filigree work.'[48] Fergusson is somewhat harsher. He begrudgingly admits the originality of the Adam brothers, but otherwise dismisses them as having 'acquired a repute for knowledge of Classical Art which their buildings by no means justify . . . When they did use Classical Orders or ornaments, they were of the thinnest and most tawdry class.'[49]

The criticisms of the Regency and early Victorian periods can be regarded as a post mortem on Adam at a time when the vogue in furniture fluctuated between the Greek, the Gothic or Elizabethan, and lavish Louis XIV Baroque or Rococo styles. After the middle of the century, however, the situation began to turn. Hints of a reaction against the current tastes for curves and plush appeared in the English entry of a Louis XVI piece by Jackson and Graham in the Paris Exhibition of 1855; in the growing preference for English, as opposed to foreign design and workmanship; in the revived interest in the delicate ornaments of Herculaneum and Pompeii, employed in a suite exhibited by Howard and Sons in the 1862 Exhibition; in the general shift of emphasis from pure comfort to 'aesthetic' and theoretical concerns; and in other contexts.[50] These trends converged in the Art Movement of the 1870s and 80s, led by E. W. Godwin, Charles Eastlake, and William Burges. Not only did the aesthetics of this period give precedence to painted decoration over carving, and to straight, slender, and simple forms over elaborate curved ones, but, more important, it admitted English eighteenth century styles as valid for imitation.

The first Adam revival was inaugurated in 1867 when the firm of Wright and Mansfield won the highest honours at the Paris Exhibition **155** for a cabinet in the Adam style. The fashion caught on immediately, and for the next forty or more years most of the leading manufacturers —Gillows, Warings, Holland and Sons, Perrys, Hamptons, Heals, **156** Hodges, and others—were producing quantities of 'Adam' furniture. In fact, the majority of the so-called 'Adam' pieces we see today date from the late nineteenth and early twentieth centuries. These are either straight forward reproductions, or free compilations of Adamesque ornaments, made with great skill, but without any real understanding of the style or its classical sources. To suit the purposes of the Art Movement, decoration was generally divorced from form, and invested with a special importance of its own. Unfortunately, it is from this work that many of the present misconceptions of the style, its association with satinwood and inlay for one, are derived.

Publishers also cashed in on the vogue. In 1880 Batsford was induced by 'The high esteem in which the decorative work of the talented Brothers is held, and the present popularity of the style in which they worked . . .' to publish a selection of plates from the *Works* under the title *The Architecture, Decoration and Furniture of Robert and James Adam.* Another pattern book, *The First Issue of Decorative Designs by Robert Adams [sic] Architect,* edited and published by R. Charles, appeared in 1883, followed in '89 by the first of the three volumes of J. Aldam Heaton's *Furniture and Decoration in England During the 18th Century,* containing facsimile reproductions of designs by Chippendale, Adam, Richardson, Hepplewhite, Sheraton, Pergolesi, and others. Responding to the continued demand for Adam designs, Batsford reissued a large folio edition of their 1880 publication in 1901, and in 1902–3 the French publisher, E. Thezard, reprinted the entire three volumes of the *Works*. In addition to the publications of authentic Adam material there were numerous pattern books of Adamesque pieces by professional furniture designers. Although these books are now extremely difficult to find intact, their circulation must have been enormous. One, for example, by A. Jonquet, a trade designer in the Queen Anne and Adam styles, was not only frequently advertised, but also partially printed in the leading trade journal, *The Cabinet Maker*.[51]

What the trade sought was not simply tasteful decoration, but adaptability on a general scale to suit a large middle-class clientele. On this count Adam fell somewhat short, especially in comparison with Chippendale and Sheraton, who were the top stars of the entire revival period. In Heaton's opinion Adam furniture was, of all things, too 'religiously devoted to those worshipful five orders,' and too much designed for rich people to be a 'really vital style which is to become traditional.'[52] Nevertheless, he was able to recommend Adam for his 'taste and discretion,' his avoidance of the 'false standards set up by a pretended admiration of classical work . . . and an extravagant desire to follow all the excesses of the French renaissance . . .', and above all because his ornament 'is capable of being executed cheaply in carton-pierre and plaster, and often forms the chaste and delicate ornamental touch of many a burgher's house, of somewhat later date.'[53] Needless to say, the original meaning of the Neo-classical style was entirely lost.

The Arts and Crafts Movement of the 1880s and 90s also gave its approval to Adam furniture, but with strong reservations on the subject of its ornament. The attitude of the defenders of the craft is expressed by Reginald Blomfield, who for a time was one of the leading designers of this group.

> . . . in so far as he introduced any innovation in detail, it was wholly for the bad, and probably little value would be placed on the furniture and

other articles carried out from his designs, except for their admirable workmanship, for skill in execution long outlasts the capacity for design in English architecture and its handicrafts.[54]

The turn of the century brought an increased interest in Adam not only from a practical, but also from an historical point of view. In practice, everything which had a swag, rams' heads, or urns, and was not Chippendale, Sheraton, or Hepplewhite, was Adam. The name was applied to objects of literally every description, and every price. For example, in 1912 one could purchase either a first-class gilded reproduction mirror from an antique specialist for not much more than £10, or an ' "Adam" bedroom suite painted white and comprising 3ft. 3in. Hanging Wardrobe, 3ft. Dressing Chest with Mirror, 3ft. Washstand Marble Top, Tiled Back Towel Rail, and 2 Cane seat chairs' from Heals for £14 14s.[55] 'Adam' was, in fact, so far removed from the works of Robert and James that in 1948 it could be defined for budding connoisseurs as a style 'derived from the modified classical revival influenced by two famous architects. . . .'[56] This is not to say that there was no discrimination between authentic and imitation pieces, but simply to illustrate the ambiguity of the term.

Oddly enough, as the market became more generalized, literature became more detailed. Batsford's folio of designs, and Thezard's reprint of the *Works* were immediately followed by the first two biographies, John Swarbrick's of 1903, and Percy Fitzgerald's of 1904. Nobody has ever been more enamoured of Adam than Fitzgerald. He extols him as a *uomo universale,* defends him against Gwilt by dismissing the idols, Stuart and Revett, as 'two rather obscure men,'[57] and in furniture design ranks him above Chippendale and Sheraton in a class 'with the Reisners and other French masters.'[58] The revival of Adam decoration he finds not very successful 'for it has been mostly copied and imitated without attempting to pierce to its true principles.'[59] To correct this error is Fitzgerald's aim, but his insight is, to say the least, rather limited. Swarbrick's account, although far from accurate, is much more palatable being of a detached and scholarly character.

His appreciation is both critical and conservative. Unlike the revivalists, he adopts the earlier nineteenth-century point of view that Adam's 'passionate admiration for richness led him to be too profuse in the application of ornament, whereby the value of the enrichment was destroyed and a sense of reticence lost.'[60]

Implacable opposition came from only one author, Herbert Cescinsky, who may be regarded as the twentieth-century counterpart of Gwilt. Cescinsky, a cabinet-maker by profession, was most disturbed by Adam's technical inefficiencies. He condemns him for being untrained, and hence unable to make the furniture he designed; for his 'reckless disregard' for materials; for producing 'sham' pieces largely of composition which, not being able to stand on its own merit, must masquerade behind gilt and paint; for his 'craze for excessive delicacy, without regard to the cardinal principle of all proportion in architecture and furniture, the sufficient appearance, as well as reality, of strength to serve the necessary purpose'; and for his 'incongruous' use of the same motifs inside and out. Furthermore, he finds Adam's 'rigid fidelity to one style' synonymous with a lack of imagination and development.[61] Right or wrong, Cescinsky's judgements are the result of an erroneous and artificial division between Adam's drawings and executed works. Whether he represents a prevalent reaction against Adam is unknown; if so, this does not enter contemporary literature. Nevertheless, his ideas could not have been entirely isolated for several are still held today, albeit by a small minority.

After World War I, the market for Adam furniture declined, but historical interest continued to advance. Although the subject was never carefully examined as a whole, Bolton's two volume monograph; a few less ambitious biographies; numerous histories of eighteenth century English furniture and interiors, notably those by Margaret Jourdain; the dictionaries of Percy Macquoid and Ralph Edwards; and countless articles on individual pieces and houses contributed a great deal of valuable information.[62] For the first two or three decades, most authors presented Adam in reasonable proportion with respect both to his French precedents, and to his influence upon Chippendale, and other English cabinet-makers. With the publication in the 1930s of Fiske Kimball's revolutionary theories on the origin of Neo-classicism,[63] Adam's image began to grow until he became the father of the 'antique' revival, the source of the Louis XVI style, and Chippendale's right-hand man.

It is hoped that the preceding chapters and following catalogue, although only a concise essay on the subject, will contribute to a better understanding of the furniture of Robert Adam.

Pier Glass in the Dining-room

Glace dans les Trumeaux de la Salle á manger

Figure e. 'Pier Glass in the Dining room' at Kenwood, 1773. 'The Works in Architecture' Vol. I, No. 2, Pl. viii (see fig. 88).

FOOTNOTES

1. Sir Joshua Reynolds, *The Discourses* (II, 1769), London, 1924, p.13.

2. John Fleming, *Robert Adam and His Circle,* London, 1962; Sir John Summerson, *Architecture in Britain* 1530–1830, London, 3rd ed., 1958, pp.248ff.; see also the analysis of Italian sources by Dr. R. Wittkower in F. Saxl and R. Wittkower, *British Art and the Mediterranean,* London, 1948, pp.72,73.

3. *The Works in Architecture of Robert and James Adam,* Vol. I, No. 1, 1773, p.3.

4. J. D. Le Roy, *Les Ruines des plus beaux Monuments de la Grèce,* Paris, 1758; James Stuart and Nicholas Revett, *The Antiquities of Athens,* Vol. I, 1762; Vol. II, 1788.

5. G. B. Piranesi, *Antichità Romane,* 1748; *Carceri,* 1750; *Trofei Di Ottaviano Augusto,* 1753.

6. Letter from Robert to James Adam, 11 December 1758, Scottish Record Office, Clerk of Penicuik Muniments, No. 4854, describing Stuart's drawings for Kedleston. Adam was equally abusive about Stuart's work at Spencer House (Fleming, *op. cit.,* p.258). In contrast to his personal comments to James, is his public statement in *The Works* (Vol. I, No. 1, 1773, p.5): 'Mr. Stuart with his usual elegance and taste has contributed greatly towards introducing the true style of antique decoration.' For a more detailed discussion of the relation between Adam and Stuart see below Notes to figures 1,2,3,6.

7. Svend Ericksen, *Lalive de Jully's Furniture 'à la grecque,'* BURLINGTON MAGAZINE, August (1961), pp.340–347; Svend Ericksen, *Marigny and Le Goût Grec,* BURLINGTON MAGAZINE, March (1962) pp.96–101; see also the furniture in Francois Hubert Drouais' portrait of Mme. de Pompadour, begun 1763 finished 1764. F. J. B. Watson, *Painter and Furniture Designer. Reflections on Taste in the Decorative Arts in France around 1760,* ANTIQUE COLLECTOR, December (1960), pp.230–231, fig. 5.

8. Baron Grimm, *Correspondance Littéraire,* Paris, 1813, Part I, Vol. III, p.362.

9. E. Harris, *Robert Adam and the Gobelins*, APOLLO, April (1962), pp.100–106; a complete and excellent account of the purchase and making of the Croome Court tapestries is given by Edith A. Standen—*Croome Court— The Tapestries*, METROPOLITAN MUSEUM OF ART BULLETIN, November (1959), pp.96–111.

10. Bills for Adam's trip to Croome, and for his designs are in his accounts to the Earl of Coventry now in the possession of the Croome Estate Trust, c.f. Standen, *Ibid*, p.107. Of the three designs mentioned, only one (Soane Vol. 50, No. 12), inscribed 'Lord Coventry's Tapestry Room,' and showing sketches of the tapestry with one wall in colour, survives. It is not clear whether this is the 'Section,' or the 'Design for Finishing the Sides'; presumably it is the latter. The sketch of the tapestry does contain Adam's alterations which, however, had no effect upon the work executed by the Gobelins.

11. Maurice Fenaille, *Etat Général des Tapisseries de la Manufacture des Gobelins*, Paris, 1907, Vol. IV, p.229.

12. *Ibid*, p.246.

13. The Earl of Coventry, William Weddell of Newby, Sir Laurence Dundas of Moor Park, Robert Child of Osterley, and the Emperor of Austria. The tapestries alone (woven before the Revolution) went to Sir Henry Bridgeman of Weston Park, Louis XVI, the Louvre, and the Grand Duke Paul Petrovich.

14. Fiske Kimball, *The Moor Park Tapestry Suite of Furniture by Robert Adam*, PHILADELPHIA MUSEUM BULLETIN, XXXVI, No. 189, March (1941), p.29; Fiske Kimball, *Les influences anglaises dans la formation du style Louis XVI*, GAZETTE DES BEAUX-ARTS, 6th ser, V (1931), p.244.

15. Bills for the Moor Park furniture are published by Arthur T. Bolton, *The Architecture of Robert and James Adam*, London, 1922, Vol. II, p.345. For the Croome Court bills see James C. Parker, *Croome Court Furniture*, METROPOLITAN MUSEUM OF ART BULLETIN, November (1959), pp.79–93.

16. Ericksen, BURLINGTON MAGAZINE, March (1962), *op. cit.*, p.98.

17. Sir John Soane's Museum, Vol. 17, No. 73, 'Sopha for Sir Laurence Dundass Bart' undated. E. Harris, *op. cit.*, p.106. The author in error referred to this design as for Arlington Street and as Adam's first Neo-classical design for furniture, the Kedleston sideboard not being known at the time of publication.

18. Quoted by Geoffrey Beard, *Robert Adam at Croome Court*, CONNOISSEUR, October (1953), p.75.

19. In 1761 a 'Mr. Anderson' exhibited at the Free Society of Artists a tripod, presumably in ormolu, '. . . from an original design of Mr. Stuart's.' (Rupert Gunnis, *Dictionary of British Sculptors,* London, 1953, p.17). This Anderson is probably the one employed by Sir William Chambers to execute bronze and ormolu objects for Lord Charlemont and other patrons in 1767. On 2 October of that year Chambers wrote to inform Charlemont that Anderson was dead. (HISTORICAL MANUSCRIPTS COMMISSION. 12th Report, Appendix, Part X. Charlemont, I, 1891, pp.283–284.)

20. Horace Walpole to Anne Pitt, 19 January 1766 and 1 March 1766. Toynbee ed., Vol. VI, pp.399–400,426. Walpole's description of the ceiling corresponds with Adam's designs Soane Vol. 11, Nos. 186,187; Vol. 50, No. 39.

21. Horace Walpole to Anne Pitt, 7 March 1766. Toynbee ed., Vol. VI, p.439. Regarding Poirier see F. J. B. Watson, *Louis XVI Furniture,* London (1960), p.79, figs. 99,122,123.

22. The second Adam sale. May 20 to 22, 1818, Lot 51. Bolton, *op. cit.,* II, p.330.

23. Josiah Wedgwood to Thomas Bentley, 15 March 1768. *Letters of Josiah Wedgwood,* ed. Lady Farrer, London, 1903, Vol. I, pp.208–9.

24. *The Works,* Vol. I, No. 1, p.6.

25. Horace Walpole to the Countess of Upper Ossory, 21 June 1773, Toynbee ed., Vol. VIII, p.292.

26. Composition: a kind of putty made of whiting, resin, glue, and linseed oil combined under heat, and when cool pressed into moulds of wood, metal, or other materials. The finished ornament is fixed in place with glue or small pins.

27. For Their Majesties, Buckingham House, *c.* 1763 (Soane, Vol. 17, Nos. 160–162); The Earl of Coventry, *c.* 1767 (Vol. 17, No. 152); Hon. F. Thynne, Curzon Street, 1772 (Vol. 17, No. 153); Lord Stanley, Derby House, Grosvenor Square, 1774 (Vol. 17, Nos. 154,155); Lady Home, Portman Square, *c.* 1775 (Vol. 14, No. 132); Robert Child, Osterley, State bed, 1775–6 (Vol. 17, Nos. 156–159); Taffeta Room bed, 1779 (Vol. 17, No. 163). Only the two beds at Osterley are known to exist.

28. Adam and his carver, John Gilbert, Ince and Mayhew, Walle & Reilty, Jno. Buhl, Thomas Chippendale, Thos. Linfoot, Thos. Vials, James Boyle, and J. Nelson all contributed to the furnishing of Lansdowne House. See Bolton, *op. cit.,* II, p.314.

29. Quoted in Bolton, *ibid,* p.312.

30. Wedgwood, *op. cit.*, I, pp.428–9. Wedgwood also reports that Giffard 'said a great deal in praise of Mr. Adams as a man of Genius & invention & an excellent architect & Mr. Freeman (of Chute Lodge, Wilts., the father of Lady Strickland) assured me that he knew Mr. Adams kept Modelers at Rome employed in copying Bas reliefs & other things for them & he thought a connection with them would be of great use of us.'

31. R. W. Symonds, *Adam and Chippendale: A Myth Exploded,* COUNTRY LIFE ANNUAL (1958), pp.53–56.

32. About half of Chippendale's bills, £3,302 from a total of £6,326 are at Harewood. Some of the bills are quoted by Symonds, *ibid,* p.56.

33. Lady Knatchbull to Robert Adam, 17 November 1774. Victoria and Albert Museum, Library. (Box VI, 86,22).

34. Chippendale to Sir Edward Knatchbull, 23 June 1778. Quoted in H. Avray Tipping, *English Homes, Late Georgian,* London, 1926, Vol. I, p. 136. The letter and bills from Chippendale are among the Mersham Papers in the possession of Lord Brabourne.

35. Symonds, *op. cit.,* p.55.

36. The present whereabouts of the original Adam furniture is unknown. It is now replaced by a suite from Spencer House, attributed to James Stuart.

37. John Gilbert's accounts for carving at Lansdowne House '. . . from March 1767 to December 1768. By order of Messrs. Adam Esq. . . .' published by Bolton, *op. cit.,* II, pp.344–5.

38. Sir William Chambers, *Treatise on the Decorative Part of Civil Architecture,* London, 3rd ed., 1791, p.132.

39. Horace Walpole to the Countess of Upper Ossory, 17 September 1785. Toynbee ed., Vol. XIII, p.321.

40. Horace Walpole to Sir Horace Mann, 22 April 1775. Toynbee ed., Vol. IX, p.186.

41. Horace Walpole to Rev. Wm. Mason, 14 February 1782. Toynbee ed., Vol. XII, p.166.

42. Horace Walpole to Rev. Wm. Mason, 29 July 1773. Toynbee ed., Vol. VIII, p. 313.

43. Sir John Soane, *Lectures on Architecture,* ed. A. T. Bolton, London 1929, Lecture XI, 16 March 1815, p.172.

44. C. H. Tatham to Henry Holland, Junior from Rome, 4 April 1796. 'The late Messrs. Adam were the children of the Arabesque, yet I do not recollect one instance in which they successfully employed it.' Instead of Adam's arabesques Tatham recommends '. . . intrinsic copies of original existing models of antiquity, rendered useful and interesting.' Soane Ms. quoted by Bolton, *op. cit.*, I, p.114.

45. *The Farington Diary,* ed. James Greig, London, 1923, Vol. II, p.180. Farington reports that in 1804 Wyatt told the King that 'When He returned from Italy He found the public taste corrupted by the Adams & He was obliged to comply with it.'

46. Joseph Gwilt, *Encyclopedia of Architecture,* London, 1842, p.226.

47. Robert Stuart (Pseud. Meikleham), *Dictionary of Architecture,* London (1830), Vol. I.

48. *The Biographical Dictionary of the Society for the Diffusion of Useful Knowledge,* London, 1842, p.285.

49. James Fergusson, *History of the Modern Styles of Architecture,* London, 1862, p.292.

50. The very brief discussion of Victorian furniture given here is greatly condensed from the wealth of material in Elizabeth Aslin, *Nineteenth Century English Furniture,* London, 1962; and R. W. Symonds and B. B. Whineray, *Victorian Furniture,* London, 1962.

51. THE CABINET MAKER, 24 November 1877, 22 June 1878, 6 July 1878.

52. John Aldam Heaton, *Furniture and Decoration in England During the 18th Century,* London, 1889, Vol. I, p.16.

53. *Ibid.,* p.16.

54. Reginald Blomfield, *A History of Renaissance Architecture in England,* London, 1897, Vol. II, p.275.

55. Heal & Son, Ltd., *The Evolution of Four Acres,* London, 1912, pp.12–13.

56. F. Gordon Roe, *Old English Furniture, Connoisseur Booklets,* London, 1948, p.11.

57. Percy Fitzgerald, *Robert Adam Artist and Architect,* London, 1904, p.15.

58. *Ibid.,* p.10.

59. *Ibid.,* p.7.

60. John Swarbrick, *The Life, Work and Influence of Robert Adam and His Brothers*, London, 1903, p.20. In 1915 Swarbrick enlarged his essay into a full size biography, eliminating most of the critical comments in the earlier book.

61. Herbert Cescinsky, *English Furniture of the Eighteenth Century*, London, 1911, Vol. III, pp.13–15.

62. See bibliography.

63. Kimball, *op. cit.*, Kimball amplifies his ideas in *The Creation of The Rococo*, Philadelphia, 1943; and *The Beginnings of the Style Pompadour 1751–9*, GAZETTE DES BEAUX-ARTS, 6th ser., XLIV (1954), pp.57–64.

SELECT BIBLIOGRAPHY

It is impossible to list all of the hundreds of books and articles in which Adam furniture is discussed. The following is a selection of the most important and useful references. COUNTRY LIFE is, of course, an invaluable source for individual houses furnished and decorated by Adam.

ADAM, Robert and James. *The Works in Architecture,* 2 vols. London, 1773–1779; third volume, 1822 (reprints: Thezard 1902; Tiranti 1939 and 1959).

BOLTON, A. T. *The Architecture of Robert and James Adam.* 2 vols. London, 1922.

EDWARDS, Ralph (ed.). *Dictionary of English Furniture.* 3 vols. 2nd ed. London, 1954.

EDWARDS, R., and JOURDAIN, M. *Georgian Cabinet-Makers.* 3rd ed. London, 1955.

ERIKSEN, Svend. *Lalive de Jully's Furniture 'à la grecque,'* BURLINGTON MAGAZINE, August 1961.

ERIKSEN, Svend. *Marigny and 'Le Goût Grec,'* BURLINGTON MAGAZINE, March 1962.

FASTNEDGE, Ralph. *English Furniture Styles from 1500 to 1830.* London, 1955.

FLEMING, John. *Robert Adam and His Circle.* London, 1962.

HARRIS, E. *Robert Adam and the Gobelins,* APOLLO, April 1962.

JOURDAIN, Margaret. *English Decoration and Furniture of the Late XVIII Century.* London, 1922.

JOURDAIN, Margaret. *English Interiors in Smaller Houses.* London, 1923.

KIMBALL, Fiske. *Les influences anglaises dans la formation du style Louis XVI,* GAZETTE DES BEAUX-ARTS. 6th ser., V., 1931.

KIMBALL, Fiske. *The Moor Park Tapestry Suite of Furniture by Robert Adam,* PHILADELPHIA MUSEUM BULLETIN, XXXVI, 189. March 1941.

KIMBALL, Fiske. *The Creation of the Rococo.* Philadelphia, 1943.

SUMMERSON, Sir John. *Architecture in Britain* 1530–1830. 3rd. ed. London, 1958.

SWARBRICK, John. *Robert Adam and His Brothers.* London, 1915.

SYMONDS, R. W. *Adam and Chippendale*: *A Myth Exploded,* COUNTRY LIFE ANNUAL, 1958.

WARD-JACKSON, Peter. *English Furniture Designs of the Eighteenth Century.* London, 1958.

WATSON, F. J. B. *Louis XVI Furniture.* London, 1961.

AN INVENTORY OF ADAM FURNITURE DESIGNS

The following list of Adam furniture designs is largely abstracted from the Topographical Index to the Collection of Adam Drawings in Sir John Soane's Museum, compiled by Walter L. Spiers, and published with notes by Arthur T. Bolton (*The Architecture of Robert and James Adam,* Vol. II). Added to Spiers' index are references to existing accounts, and to drawings in other collections both public and private. Some of the many uninscribed drawings in the Soane have also been identified and incorporated. Although every effort has been made to record all of the known designs and accounts, the inventory does not pretend to be definitive, but is merely intended as an aid to those interested in pursuing the study of Adam furniture.

Attributed dates and places are given in parentheses. The letter S is used throughout to refer to the Soane Museum.

PLACE AND SUBJECT	NAME OF CLIENT DATE OF DESIGN	LOCATION OF DESIGNS AND ACCOUNTS
ALNWICK CASTLE, Northumberland	*Duke of Northumberland*	
Carpet, Chapel	1780	S. 17(201–202)
Gothic Chair, Chapel	(1761)	S. 50(21), cf. Croome Court
Gothic Mirror, Stove, and Lectern, Chapel	(*c.* 1780)	Alnwick
(*ALWALTON, Hunts.*)	*John Kenrick*	
Mirrors	1783	S. 20(246–249)

AUDLEY END, Essex — Sir John Griffin Griffin

PLACE AND SUBJECT	DATE OF DESIGN	LOCATION OF DESIGNS AND ACCOUNTS
Picture Frames	1764	Essex Record Office Accounts
Pedestals	1765	S. 17(59); Audley End Scrap Book p.53; Essex Record Office
Mirrors	1765, 1771	Audley End Scrap Book pp. 55, 60; Essex Record Office
Curtain Cornices	1766, 1771	Essex Record Office
Tables	1769	S. 52(111); Essex Record Office
Stools	1771	Audley End Scrap Book p.60;
Settee	1771	Essex Record Office

BOWOOD, Wilts. — Earl of Shelburne

Mirror	1765	S. 20(19)

BRASTED PLACE, Kent — Dr. John Turton

Mirrors		S. 3(8,12)

BRIGHTON, Sussex — Rt. Hon. William Gerald Hamilton

Sideboard and wine cistern		S. 6(116,118), 17(225)
Carpet		S. 17(211)

BRODSWORTH, Yorks. — Archbishop of York

Table	1768	S. 17(11)

BYRAM, Yorks. — Sir John Ramsden, Bt. (c. 1780)

Sideboard, pedestals and urns		S. 25(156)
Hall Chair		S. 24(182), 17(100–104)
Mirror		S. 23(151)
Term and lamp		S. 17(68)
Carpet		S. 17(209)

CASTLE HOUSE, Wilts. — Daniel Bull

Mirror		S. 20(91)
Mirror and table	1771	S. 20(92)

CHILLINGTON PARK, Staffs. — Thomas Giffard (c. 1772)

Table (detail)		S. 5(37)

COMBE BANK, Kent — Lord Frederick Campbell

Bookcase	1767	S. 17(215)
Mirror and commode	1767	S. 20(31)

CORSHAM COURT, Wilts.
  Mirror, Picture Gallery — Paul Methuen — 1767 — S. 20(55); Corsham
  Mirror, Cabinet Room — 1771–2 — S. 20(56,57); Corsham
  Picture and mirror frames
    (details) — S. 5(34)
  Girandole — 1772 — S. 20(58); Corsham
  Table — 1771 — S. 20(57); Corsham

Place and Subject	Client / Date	Location
CORSHAM COURT, Wilts.	*Paul Methuen*	
Mirror, Picture Gallery	1767	S. 20(55); Corsham
Mirror, Cabinet Room	1771–2	S. 20(56,57); Corsham
Picture and mirror frames (details)		S. 5(34)
Girandole	1772	S. 20(58); Corsham
Table	1771	S. 20(57); Corsham
(COWORTH HOUSE, Berks.)	*Mr. Nettleship*	
Mirror	1784	S. 20(256)
CROOME COURT, Worcs.	*Earl of Coventry*	
Clothes Press	1764	S. 17(212–213); Croome Accounts
Window Stool	(1764–5)	S. 17(73); Croome Accounts; cf. *Moor Park*
Chairs	1761, 1765	S. 50(21); 6(159,161); Croome Accounts
Table	1765	S. 17(4); cf. *Syon*
Tripod Pedestals	1767	S. 6(177); Croome Accounts; *Works,* I–I–viii
Bed		S. 17(152)
CULLEN, Banffshire	*Earl of Findlater*	
Mirror	1781	S. 20(226), 23(167)
Mirror and table	1781	S. 20(225,250)
CULZEAN CASTLE, Ayrshire	*Earl of Cassillis*	
Mirrors	1782	S. 20(228,231–234)
Girandole	1782	S. 20(236)
DUPPLIN CASTLE, Perthshire	*Earl of Kinnoull*	
Mirrors	1768, 1769	S. 3(39), 20(221–223)
EDINBURGH	*Mr. John Adam*	
Mirrors	1772	S. 3(15,19,38,95)
EDINBURGH, 8 Queen Street	*Lord Chief Baron Ord*	
Chair seat and back		S. 49(50,52)
EPSOM, Surrey	*Anthony Chamier*	
Mirrors	1776	S. 20(152–154)

E

PLACE AND SUBJECT	NAME OF CLIENT DATE OF DESIGN	LOCATION OF DESIGNS AND ACCOUNTS
GREAT SAXHAM, Suffolk	*Hutchinson Mure*	
Mirrors	1776	S. 20(157,158)
Carpet	1775	S. 17(193)
Organ Case	1775	S. 25(14)
KEDLESTON, Derbyshire	*Lord Scarsdale*	
Tripod Candelabrum	(*c.* 1761)	S. 25(89–91)
Wine Cooler	(*c.* 1761)	S. 25(80)
Urns and basin	(*c.* 1761)	S. 25(83)
Plate Warmer	(*c.* 1761)	S. 25(91–93)
Sideboard, plan and elevations	1762	Kedleston
Pedestal	(1762)	Kedleston
Sofa	1762	S. 17(69)
Mirrors	1765, (*c.* 1767?)	S. 20(8), 40(15)
Girandole	1767	S. 20(9)
Carpet		S. 17(164–5), 54(7,37)
Organ Case		S. 25(1–3); Kedleston
KENWOOD, Middlesex	*Lord Mansfield*	
Mirrors	(1767–8), (1769–70)	
	1773	*Works* I-II-viii; *Works* I-II-v, S. 3(31), Kenwood Accounts; S. 20(119,120)
Sofa	(1768–9)	S. 6(151), Kenwood Accounts
Window Stool	(1768–9)	S. 3(31), Kenwood Accounts
Sideboard, pedestals, and urns	(1768–9)	*Works* I–II–viii
Term		S. 6(69), 54(260)
Curtain Cornices	(1768–9)	Kenwood Accounts
KIMBOLTON CASTLE, Hunts.	*Duke of Manchester*	
Mirror	1765	S. 20(28)
Cabinet	1771	S. 17(218)
KIPPINGTON PARK, Kent	*Sir Charles Farnaby*	
Table	1765	S. 17(6)
LUTON PARK, Beds.	*Earl of Bute*	
Mirror, table, and pedestals	1772	S. 20(116), *Works* III-viii
Mirrors	1772	S. 20(112–115)
Table	1772	S. 17(19)
Girandole		S. 6(29)
Organ Case	1763	S. 25(4,5)
MISTLEY, Essex	*Rt. Hon. Richard* *Rigby*	
Mirrors	1778	S. 20(180–184)
Carpet	1778	S. 5(43), 17(198)

PLACE AND SUBJECT	NAME OF CLIENT DATE OF DESIGN	LOCATION OF DESIGNS AND ACCOUNTS
MITCHAM, Surrey	*John Stewart*	
Mirror	1771	S. 20(80)
MOOR PARK, Herts.	*Sir Laurence Dundas*	
Window Stool	(*c.* 1764–5)	S. 17(73); Accounts-Bolton II, 345; see *Croome Court*
Sofas	(*c.* 1765)	S. 6(152), 17(71–2)
'Patterns of Bed Carpet and Sewed Chairs'	(*c.* 1765)	Accounts–Bolton II, 345
NEWBY HALL, Yorks.	*William Weddell*	
Mirrors	1770	S. 3(27), 20(77–79)
Table and slab	1775	S. 17(32), 49(40)
Sideboard		S. 6(115,140)
Wine Cooler		S. 17(226)
Commode		S. 24(230)
Carpet	1775	S. 17(194)
NOSTELL PRIORY, Yorks.	*Sir Rowland Winn, Bt.*	
Tables and slab	1775	S. 17(27–8), 49(42)
Picture frame	1773	S. 20(117)
OSTERLEY PARK, Middlesex	*Robert Child*	
Mirrors	1767–77	S. 18(64), 20(23,34,35,42–9); Osterley
Girandole	1767, 1770	S. 3(35), 20(32,33,36,37)
Curtain Cornices	1768, 1776	S. 17(105–7)
Sideboard, pedestals, and urns	1767	S. 17(7); *Works* III–ix; Osterley
Tables	1775, 1777	S. 17(8), 20(49)
Commode	1773	S. 5(20,21), 18(63), 25(210)
Beds	1775–7, 1779	S. 17(156–9,163), 6(112)
Pedestal	1776	S. 17(62)
Chairs	1776–7	S. 17(93,95–7)
Fire Screens	1776–9	S. 17(133–6,141–5,148–9), 5(36), 24(233)
Work Bag	1776	S. 17(140)
Carpets	1775–78	S. 17(186–192)
PAINS HILL, Surrey	*Hon. Charles Hamilton*	
Pedestal	(*c.* 1761–2)	S. 54(53)
(*PATSHULL, Staffs.*)	*Sir John Astley*	
Pedestal	1765	S. 17(58)

PLACE AND SUBJECT	NAME OF CLIENT DATE OF DESIGN	LOCATION OF DESIGNS AND ACCOUNTS
SALTRAM, Devon	*John Parker, 1st* *Lord Boringdon*	S. 20(69,70,235,237); Saltram
Mirrors	1769, 1771, 1781	Accounts
		S. 20(70); Saltram Accounts
Table	1771	S. 25(158,159)
Pedestal and urn	1780	S. 8(99), 17(178)
Carpet	1769	
SHARDELOES, Bucks.	*William Drake*	Drake papers—Bucks. County
Sideboard, pedestals, and urns	1767	Record Office
SYON HOUSE, Middlesex	*Duke of Northum-* *berland*	S. 20(14–6); *Works* III–xi
Mirrors	1765	S. 17(1–4); *Works* III–xi; Syon
Tables	1765	House Book 1769.
		S. 17(171,172)
Carpets	1768	
WEALD HALL, Essex	*Christopher Towers*	S. 17(54)
Table	1779	S. 17(116)
Curtain Cornice	1779	
WELWYN, Herts.	*Mrs. St. John*	S. 3(45)
Mirror (sketch)	*(c. 1775)*	
WIMBLEDON, Surrey	*Sir Ellis and Sir* *Foster Cunliffe,* *Bts.*	S. 20(50–4)
Mirrors	1767	S. 49(59)
Pedestal and urn	*(c. 1778)*	
(WOOLBEDING HOUSE, Sussex)	*Lord Robert Spen-* *cer*	S. 3(64)
Mirror and table		
WORMLEYBURY, Herts.	*Sir Abraham Hume,* *Bt.*	
Sideboard, pedestals, urns, and wine cooler	1778	S. 17(34) S. 17(197)
Carpet	1778	

LONDON HOUSES

PLACE AND SUBJECT	NAME OF CLIENT DATE OF DESIGN	LOCATION OF DESIGNS AND ACCOUNTS
ADLEPHI, Adam Street	*Messrs. Adam*	
Mirrors	1772	S. 20(97–9), 3(82,83); *Works* I–I–viii
Table	(1772)	*Works* I–I–viii
ADELPHI	*George Hesse*	
Mirrors	1779	S. 20(210–3,239)
Girandoles		S. 20(211,238), 6(14)
Carpet	1779	S. 17(200)
ARLINGTON STREET, No. 19	*Sir Laurence Dundas*	
Sofa	1764	S. 17(74); Accounts Bolton II,345
Chair	(1764)	*En suite* with sofa
Table	1765	S. 17(5); Accounts Bolton II, 345
Mirrors	1765	S. 20(11–13); Accounts Bolton II,345
Term	(1765)	Accounts Bolton II,345
China Cupboard	1766	S. 17(214); Accounts Bolton II, 345
Tripod Candelabrum	(*c.* 1768)	*Works* I–I–viii
ARLINGTON STREET, No. (23)	*Sir George Colebrooke, Bt.*	
Bookcase	1771	S. 17(219)
Commode	1771	S. 17(17)
Toilet Table	1771	S. 17(16)
Sofa		S. 50(54)

PLACE AND SUBJECT	NAME OF CLIENT DATE OF DESIGN	LOCATION OF DESIGNS AND ACCOUNTS
LANSDOWNE HOUSE, Berkeley *Square*	*Earl of Shelburne* 1768	S. 3(40,87,88); 17(12–5), 20(24–6); Bowood; *Works* II–III–viii; Accounts Bolton II,340,345
Tables		
Mirrors	1768–9	S. 3(38,40,87,88), 20(20–7); Accounts Bolton II,340,345
Stool	1768	S. 17(76)
Sofa	1769	S. 17(75)
Cabinet	1770	S. 17(216)
Pedestal and urn	(1768)	Accounts Bolton II,340
Carpets	1769	S. 17(174–7)
BERKELEY SQUARE, No. 38	*Robert Child*	
Cabinet	1768	S. 17(217)
Mirrors	1770, 1771	S. 6(103), 20(38–41); Osterley
Girandole		Osterley
Table and mirror		Osterley
BUCKINGHAM HOUSE, St. *James's*	*Their Majesties*	
Bed		S. 17(160–2)
Pianoforte (sketch)	1780	S. 49(2–5)
CHARING CROSS, Drummond's *Bank*	*Messrs. Drummond*	
Mirror and table	1779	S. 20(209)
Table	1779	S. 17(55)
CHARLOTTE STREET	*George Keate*	
Mirrors	1772–3, 1777	S. 20(104–110), 23(104,245)
Girandoles	1772	S. 20(102,103)
Table	1777	S. 17(33)
Commode and mirror	1778	S. 20(109,110)
CURZON STREET, No. (30)	*Hon. F. Thynne*	
Mirrors	1771	S. 3(46,62), 20(94,95,193–5)
Bed	1772	S. 17(153)
DOVER STREET, No. 19	*Earl of Ashburnham*	
Sideboard, pedestals, urns and wine cooler	1774	S. 17(23)
Mirrors	1774–6	S. 20(139–146)
Term	1774	S. 6(66), 17(61)
Tripod Pedestal		S. 6(64)

PLACE AND SUBJECT	NAME OF CLIENT DATE OF DESIGN	LOCATION OF DESIGNS AND ACCOUNTS
GREAT GEORGE STREET, No. 28	Lord Chief Baron Eyre	
Mirrors		S. 3(1,4,14)
GREAT GEORGE STREET	Henry Drummond	
Girandole	1781	S. 6(39), 20(224)
Pedestal	1781	S. 17(67)
GROSVENOR SQUARE, No. 23	Lord Stanley, 12th	
Derby House	Earl of Derby	
Mirrors	1774, 1777	S. 20(133–7), 23(46,51), 24(173); *Works* II–I–iii,iv,v, vi.
Girandoles	1774	S. 6(41,97), 20(138); *Works* II–I–viii
Curtain Cornices	1774	S. 17(108–113); *Works* II–I–viii
Bed	1774	S. 17(154,155)
Chairs	1774, 1775	S. 6(155–8), 17(94)
Sofa	1774	S. 17(81)
Commode	1774	S. 17(24–6), 52(4); *Works* II–I–viii
Picture Frame		S. 54(267)
Carpets	1775	S. 17(184,185)
GROSVENOR SQUARE, No. 18	Earl of Thanet	
Mirrors	1764	S. 20(1–5)
Girandole	1764	S. 20(6)
GROSVENOR SQUARE	Sir Robert Rich, Bt.	
Mirrors	1770	S. 20(75,76)
HANOVER SQUARE, Roxburgh	Duke of Roxburgh	
(later Harewood) House		
Curtain Cornices	1779	S. 17(114–5)
Table and slabs	1779	S. 17(49–51)
Tables and mirrors	1779	S. 20(215,216)
Mirrors	1779	S. 20(214,217–220)
Pedestal	1779	S. 17(66)
HERTFORD STREET, No. 10	General Burgoyne	
Girandole	1771	S. 20(87)
Mirrors	1771	S. 20(88,89)
Picture Frame	1771	S. 20(90)

HILL STREET, No. 31 — Sir Abraham Hume, Bt.

Tables and slabs	1779	S. 20(202,206), 17(36–42)
Mirrors	1779	S. 20(202,203,205,206)
Girandole	1779	S. 6(26), 20(204)
Picture Frame	1779	S. 20(207)
Chairs	1778, 1779	S. 6(160,162), 17(86,98)
Chair backs and seats	1778–79	S. 17(88–90)
Sofas	1779	S. 17(84,85)
Confident	1780	S. 17(83)
Tripod Candelabrum	1779	S. 17(65)
Curtain Cornice	1779	S. 17(117), 52(78)
Carpet	1779	S. 5(45), 17(199)

HILL STREET — Mrs. Montagu

Chair bottom	(*c.* 1766)	S. 49(51)
Carpet	(*c.* 1766)	S. 17(166,167)

KENSINGTON GORE — Miss Anne Pitt

Mirror	1770	S. 20(81)

MANSFIELD STREET, No. 22 — Sir Edward Dering, Bt.

Mirrors	1775	S. 3(25), 20(148–151)
Tables	1775	S. 17(29–31)

MANSFIELD STREET — Lord Scarsdale

Mirror	1772	S. 20(10)
Sofas		Kedleston

NEW BURLINGTON STREET — Sir John Griffin Griffin

Mirror and commode	1778	S. 20(199)
Pedestal		S. 54(269)

NEW PALACE YARD, Westminster — Samuel Remnant

Mirrors	1782	S. 20(229,230)

NORTHUMBERLAND HOUSE — Duke of Northumberland

Mirrors	1773	S. 20(17,18), 39(5–7); Northumberland Accounts
Table Slab	1774	S. 39(8)
Carpet	1774	S. 17(173)

PALL MALL, Cumberland House	*H.R.H. the Duke of Cumberland*	
Sideboard, pedestals, urns and wine cooler	1780	S. 17(57)
Table and slab		S. 17(56), 49(28)
Curtain Cornice	1780	S. 17(118,119)
Carpets	1780	S. 17(202–7)
Organ Case	1781	S. 25(16–19)
Fire Screen	1782	S. 17(144,150,151)
PICCADILLY, Apsley House	*Lord Bathurst*	
Mirrors	1778	S. 20(168–175)
Girandoles	1778	S. 20(176–9)
Sofas	1778	S. 17(82), 20(178)
Chairs		S. 6(163)
Chair back (sketch)	1778	S. 17(99)
Commode	1777, 1779	S. 17(35,43) V. & A. E. 3225–1938
Tables and slabs	1779	S. 17(44–48), 49(43–46)
Pedestals	1779	S. 17(64,169), 6(49,50,52)
PICCADILLY, No. 29	*Earl of Coventry*	
Table	1767	S. 17(10)
Chair	1767	S. 6(158), 17(92)
Mirrors	1768–70	S. 20(59,60,62–66,68)
Girandoles	(1768)	S. 20(61,67)
Picture Frame (sketch)		S. 7(133)
Carpets	1767	S. 5(78), 18(57), 17(169,170)
PORTLAND PLACE, No. 66	*Mrs. Cornwall*	
Mirror	1783	S. 23(161)
(PORTLAND PLACE, No. 37)	*Lord Stormont*	
Mirrors	1778	S. 20(185–192)
PORTMAN SQUARE, No. 20	*Countess of Home*	
Bed	*(c. 1776)*	S. 6(110), 14(132)
Mirrors	1775, 1777	S. 50(34), 20(163–7)
Picture Frame		S. 20(162)
Pedestals	1778	S. 17(63), 54(265)
Fire Screen		S. 25(217)
Organ Case	1775	S. 25(15)
Carpet	1776	S. 17(195,196)

PLACE AND SUBJECT	NAME OF CLIENT DATE OF DESIGN	LOCATION OF DESIGNS AND ACCOUNTS
RUSSELL SQUARE, Bolton House	*Duke of Bolton*	
Girandole	1771	S. 20(86)
Mirrors	1772	S. 20(82–5)
Commode	1773	S. 17(18)
Sofa	1773	S. 17(80)
Tripod Candelabrum	(*c.* 1771)	*Works* I–I–viii
ST. JAMES'S SQUARE, No. 20	*Sir Watkin Williams Wynne, Bt.*	
Sideboard	1773	S. 17(20,21)
Table	1773	S. 17(22)
Pedestals	1773, 1777	S. 6(53,54), 17(60); Accounts. National Museum of Wales
Mirrors	1773	S. 20(121–132)
Girandoles	1774	S. 6(38,84)
Bookcase	1776	S. 17(220–2), 23(239); Accounts National Museum of Wales
Carpet	1773	S. 17(181–3)
ST. JAMES'S STABLE YARD	*Earl of Harrington*	
Mirrors	1773	S. 20(118), 23(15)
ST. MARTIN'S LANE	*Mr. Hamilton*	
Mirror		S. 3(36,97)
SOHO SQUARE, No. 20	*Hon. Baron Grant*	
Carpet	1772	S. 17(179,180)
TOWER OF LONDON	*Mr. Weaver*	
Mirrors	1783	S. 20(240–5)
WIMPOLE STREET	*Major Mayne (later Lord Newhaven)*	
Mirrors	1771	S. 20(100–1)

UNKNOWN

PLACE AND SUBJECT	NAME OF CLIENT DATE OF DESIGN	LOCATION OF DESIGNS AND ACCOUNTS
	Mrs. Bannister	
Mirror and Girandole	1777	S. 20(159)
	Peter Drinkwater	
Mirror	1779	S. 20(208)
	Matthew Duane	
Mirrors	1774	S. 3(78,90), 20(147)
	Mr. President Dundas	
Sofa	1770	S. 6(147), 17(77)
	Marquess of Granby	
Picture Frame	1772	S. 20(111)
	Sir Thomas Halifax	
Mirror and Girandole	1777	S. 20(160,161)
	Mr. Macdonald	
Bookcase		S. 17(223)
	Lady Betty Macfarland	
Mirror and Girandole	1765	S. 20(7)
	Lady Mills	
Fire Screen	1778	S. 17(147), 25(216)
Girandole	1775	S. 6(30)
	John Luke Niccol	
Mirrors	1766	S. 20(29,30)
	Lady Elizabeth Stanley	
Fire Screen		S. 3(73)
	Dr. Warren	
Mirrors	1776	S. 20(155,156)
Girandole	1776	S. 6(15)
	Mr. Wood	
Mirror	1783	S. 20(251,252)

NOTES TO THE ILLUSTRATIONS

The following notes are concerned primarily with the significance of each object in the development of the Adam style. They are prefaced by the measurements given in centimetres, and a brief description of the materials and colour. In the case of drawings and engravings, dates and inscriptions are given in full as they appear. References to related designs and accounts are quoted wherever known.

The plates are divided into eight groups: 1. Tables; 2. Cabinets and commodes; 3. Mirrors; 4. Oval mirrors and girandoles; 5. Seat furniture; 6. Beds; 7. Pedestals; 8. Attributed pieces, copies, and 'Adam' style furniture. Combined units of mirrors, and tables or commodes, which could not be divided are placed either in the category of the more important piece, or where needed to complete a logical sequence. When units have been separated, cross references are always given to the related part. The articles within each group (except for the last) are arranged chronologically.

In order to illustrate a particular point, some pieces by other makers are grouped with Adam's rather than in the general category of 'Adam' style furniture. Classical objects are always placed in proximity to the Adam version. The tripod candle-stand (fig. 6), although not considered furniture, is included both as an example of one of Adam's first efforts in Neo-classical design, and as an important element in the discussion of his sources.

While Adam furniture begins as independent or movable articles, some pieces, especially mirrors and girandoles, are later assimilated into the wall decorations. I am fully aware that, taken out of their original context, such pieces lose something, and at the same time gain an importance and individuality which was not intended. The reader should take this into account. To compensate for the obvious necessity of reproducing individual items, I have made a point of describing, whenever possible, the relationship of the object to its surroundings.

1. DESIGN FOR A WINDOW PIER attributed to James Stuart. Viscount Scarsdale, Kedleston Hall.

Pen and ink and water-colour. Approximate size H: 36cm.; W: 55cm. Detail from a section through a Great Hall of two stories and five bays. The section does not correspond to any of the rooms shown on either James Paine's or Adam's plans for Kedleston. It is therefore suggested that it may relate to an earlier project for the new house *c.* 1757 by Matthew Brettingham. There is an elevation at Kedleston for a house of 13 bays with a five bay columned centrepiece and an arched entrance, which would appear to fit this section. The interior design is attributed to Stuart on the basis of stylistic similarities with the drawing for Spencer House (fig. 2), and because Stuart is known to have been employed for the decoration of Kedleston before 1758. On 11 December 1758 Robert Adam wrote to his brother James (Clerk of Penicuik Muniments No. 4854. Scottish Record Office, Edinburgh) '. . . Sir Nathaniel brought me out a Design of the Great Athenians for his Rooms finishing, which he beg'd me for Godsake not to Mention to any Body. They are so excessively & so ridiculously bad, that Mr. Curson [sic] immediately saw the folly of them & said so to some people which so offended the proud Grecian, that he has not seen Sr. Nathaniel these 2 Years, and he says he keeps the Drawings Sacred in Self defence . . .'. According to Adam's gossip, Stuart's designs were made late in 1756, or, more likely, early in 1757. He goes on to describe one design for '. . . Tables of 2 foot Sqr. in a Room of 50 foot long with belts of Stone & great pannels & Roses & festoon & figures all Ramm'd in wherever there was a hole to be got for them. . .' Is this, in fact, an exaggerated description of the section of the room which, according to the scale given, is 50 feet long, and does have tables two feet wide, roses, festoons, panels (not great), and figures all rather isolated one from the other rather than 'Ramm'd in'? This section is the only design at Kedleston, which contains furniture, and can be attributed to Stuart. No matter how pitiful the tables might have appeared to Adam, if drawn in 1757 they are extremely advanced examples of Neoclassicism, contemporary with Lalive de Jully's furniture, and with the earliest designs published by Neufforge. Especially interesting for the influence which Stuart's classicism might have had on Adam, his successor at Kedleston, is the tripod candle-stand which upon close examination can be found to be of the same type as that designed by Adam *c.* 1760–61 for the Kedleston sideboard composition (fig. 3). The pedestals at the sides of the table are similar in shape to those almost certainly by Stuart for Spencer House, St. James's (now at Althorp, see fig. 152). Stuart's designs for Kedleston are among his very first works following his return from Greece in 1755.

2. DESIGN FOR THE PAINTED ROOM AT SPENCER HOUSE, ST. JAMES'S.

James Stuart. British Museum Print Room. Pen and ink and water-colour. H: 28cm; W: 40.3cm. Detail from a section of an entrance wall. The date MDCCLVIIII appears in a tablet over the door. Note the simple classicizing table frame with straight fluted legs and paw feet. The large lion underneath is an extremely unusual detail possibly of antique origin, but more characteristic of the Regency period than the mid 18th century. The tripod candle-stand with crudely drawn female heads is the same as the one in the earlier Kedleston drawing (fig. 1) and in the later design by Adam (fig. 3). A sketch by Adam of a 'Cornice in the South Dressing-Room of Mr. Spencer's House by Mr. S.' (Soane Vol. 54, No. 40) before 1761 when Mr. Spencer was created Lord Spencer, indicates that he was familiar with Stuart's work.

3. 'DRAWING AT LARGE OF THE SIDE-BOARD IN THE NICH [sic] OF THE DINING ROOM AT KEDLESTON.'

Viscount Scarsdale, Kedleston Hall.
Pen and ink and grey wash. H: 44.3cm; W: 58cm. Inscribed with title, signed and dated 'Robt. Adam Architect 1762.' The Kedleston album also contains a ground plan of the sideboard, and a coloured section of '. . . the West end of the Dining Room with the niche and sideboard,' both dated 1762. The composition includes three curved tables, separated by two tall pedestals supporting urns fitted with spouts which empty into basins on lower round pedestals, and a large sarcophagus-like wine cooler shown only in the ground plan. Drawings in the Soane for the wine cooler (Vol. 25, No. 80), the tripod candle-stand (Vol. 25, Nos. 89, 91), and the two urns and basins (Vol. 25, No. 83), each inscribed 'For Sir Nathaniel Curzon Baronet' indicate that the accessories were designed before 9 April 1761, approximately a year or more before the table. These objects, and especially the plate mounts to the knife cases, are remarkably advanced for their date. To what extent their design had already been determined by James Stuart is an extremely interesting and puzzling problem. The similarity between Adam's tripod candle-stand and those in Stuart's earlier designs for Kedleston and Spencer House (figs. 1, 2) is unmistakable. In addition, A. T. Bolton, who surely knew the Adam drawings in the Soane inside out, reports, in spite of the drawing noted above, that the wine cooler of Sicilian jasper (see fig. 4) is 'said to have been designed by Stuart.' (Bolton I, p.241.) Neither Bolton nor Christopher Hussey, who is even more precise in attributing the piece to 'J. Stuart' (*English Country Houses Mid Georgian*, London, 1956, p.77), connected this Stuart with James or 'Athenian' Stuart for that fact has only just emerged with the publication of John Fleming's biography based upon the Adam correspondence. With Bolton's comment, the Adam letters, and the Kedleston and Spencer House designs, the possibility that Adam redrew, perfected, and incorporated Stuart's ideas becomes more than a wild hypothesis.

The Kedleston sideboard is one of Adam's earliest efforts as a furniture designer, preceded, as far as we know, only by the Gothic chair at Alnwick (fig. 96). It is also his first piece in the Neo-classical style. Although Neo-classical furniture was known in France at the latest by 1757, and had already been designed by Stuart, also since *c.* 1757 (figs. 1, 2), there appear to be no precedents for this particular kind of assemblage. The influence of Adam's Roman experience is unmistakable, and indeed is much fresher here than in many of his later works. The combination of various pieces and objects seems spiritually akin to the picturesque congeries of antique fragments which were the delight of most late eighteenth century artists in

Rome, especially Piranesi and Clérisseau. The design is essentially a pictorial one, in other words it is much more effective on paper than in execution. Adam's later sideboard compositions (figs. 15,19,25,34,35) are less dramatic, but more successful as furniture.

4. SIDEBOARD IN THE NICHE OF THE DINING ROOM. Kedleston Hall, Derbyshire.

The niche painted pale blue with the ornaments above picked out in white. The tables white with gold detail and marble tops; the wine cooler of Sicilian jasper. There is at Kedleston an abstract of part of an original bill giving the costs of the tables, and the pedestals (now removed to other parts of the house) as follows: 'To 3 rich crescent table frames £13 8s.; To 2 oval pedestals for silver cisterns £6; To 2 square pedestals for silver urns £1 4s.' The maker, however, is unknown. Two additional silver mounted mahogany knife boxes (only four of the eight shown in the drawing appear to have been executed), the chased ormolu tripod candle-stand, and the two small metal urns with gilt brass ornaments (shown in the foreground of the drawing) now decorated other pieces in the Dining Room. The large spouting urns, and the cisterns or basins shown in the design are not known to have been executed. According to a description given by Margaret Jourdain in 1912 (*The Works of Robert Adam, Kedleston*, ART JOURNAL, February 1912, pp.68–69), the tall square pedestals were surmounted by the small metal urns described above. Although the composition seems grandiose on paper, in reality it is rather dwarfed in the large niche. The effect might have been somewhat more compact had the vault been as richly coloured (bright red, blue, green, and gold) as it is in Adam's section. Even so, the expanse of wall behind, left blank by Adam (the present mirror and girandoles have been added since 1912, and were not designed by Adam), calls for some furniture or decoration to integrate the cove of the niche and the tables and objects below.

5. SIDEBOARD TABLE. Kedleston Hall, Derbyshire. Dining Room.

H: 81cm; W: (corner to corner) front—75cm; rear—113cm; D: 59.5cm.   Carved wood painted white with details picked out in gold; the top of marble. One of three tables forming a curved sideboard, the centre one slightly larger (W: front—106cm; rear—155cm). Executed with minor alterations from Adam's design dated 1762. In the window piers of the Dining Room are two larger rectangular side tables with the same straight, fluted legs, and friezes of half patera and swags. Except for the addition of segmental patera joining the legs to the frieze, and festoon drops issuing from the rosettes in the capitals, these tables are more faithful to Adam's design than the curved ones which lack small details like the foliate enrichments at the feet, and the short drops between each swag on the frieze. Furthermore, they are considerably richer in effect, having the additional ornaments, being entirely gilded, and executed in slightly higher relief. Although no specific drawing exists, it can be safely concluded that they were also designed by Adam.

6. PERFUME BURNER.   Victoria and Albert Museum.

H: 53.9cm. Cast and chased ormolu on marble plinth. From Wentworth Woodhouse, Yorks. The piece corresponds exactly to a design by Adam (Soane Vol. 25, No. 90) inscribed 'Tripod for Sir Nathaniel Curzon, Bart.,' thus datable before 9 April 1761. This design was rejected by Curzon (later Lord Scarsdale) for another (Soane Vol. 25, Nos. 89,91) similarly inscribed and identical in every detail except for the addition of candle branches. The Kedleston candle-stick is included in Adam's design for the Dining Room side board 1762 (fig. 3). A remarkably similar tripod with female heads and paw feet appears in James Stuart's earlier designs for Kedleston *c.* 1757 (fig. 1) and Spencer House, 1759 (fig. 2). A pair of tripods identical to those at the Victoria and Albert Museum, and at Kedleston, but with nine instead of three candle branches was executed for the pedestals designed by James Stuart for Spencer House (fig. 152). Oddly enough the Victoria and Albert Museum perfume burner also comes from a house in which Stuart was employed, before 1768. The pieces may have a specific classical model which has not been identified.

In any event, it would seem that the idea was first conceived by Stuart, improved by Adam, and accepted by the patrons of both men. The traditional attribution of this family of tripods to Matthew Boulton is by no means convincing, for there is no concrete evidence of Boulton having produced any ormolu until after the opening of his Soho manufactory in 1762. On the other hand, we do know that a tripod, designed by Stuart and executed by Mr. Anderson, the bronze founder employed by Sir William Chambers, was exhibited at the Free Society of Artists in 1761 (see above footnote No. 19). Thus, it is altogether possible that it was Mr. Anderson who executed these pieces.

Of the numerous types of tripods derived from Roman sacrificial altars, this particular pattern was one of Adam's favourites which he employed not only as a decorative object but also as a two-dimensional ornament for stucco and painted decorations, on walls, mirror crests, friezes, etc. It was not, however, until after 1767 that the classical form was translated into a full scale article of furniture (fig. 134).

7. 'DESIGN OF A TABLE FRAME FOR THE TWO PORPHYRY TABLES: END OF THE TABLE FRAME.' Sir John Soane's Museum. Vol. 17, No. 6.

Pen and ink and grey wash. H: 26.7cm; W: 37.2cm. Inscribed with title, signed and dated 1765. The name of the client, Sir Charles Farnaby, added in pencil. Presumably for Kippington Park, Kent, for which Adam designed several chimney pieces in 1764, but no other furniture or decoration. The inscription suggests that the table was specially designed to receive the porphyry slabs. Whether it was executed is not known. The design is a bolder, and more classicized version of the Kedleston sideboard of 1762 (fig. 3). It is, in fact, the most severely classical of all of Adam's tables.

8. CONSOLE TABLE. Formerly The Marquess of Zetland.

W: 167.6cm. Carved and gilt wood with semi-circular green marble top. Executed for Sir Laurence Dundas, 19 Arlington Street, from a design dated 1765 (Soane, Vol. 17, No. 5). The design is described in Adam's bill of 18 July 1765 as '. . . a Table Frame for Long Room next the Eating Parlour £5 5s.' (Bolton II, p.345.) A similar table with a frieze of guilloche and rosettes, a fluted stretcher, and a plinth band of scroll and anthemion motifs has been unconvincingly described as a pair with this. (Ralph Edwards. *Dictionary of English Furniture*. Vol. III. 1954 fig. 63, pp.296,299.) It would seem more likely that the variant piece was executed at the same date and by the same cabinet-maker (Samuel Norman?) for Sir Laurence's country seat, Moor Park. The two tables would have become paired in 1784 when Moor Park was sold and its furnishings moved to Arlington Street. Both examples reveal the influence of Kentian tradition upon Adam's early work. A similar design made in 1768 for Lansdowne (then Shelburne) House (fig. 18) illustrates the rapid development of Adam's style in the short period of three years. The goat's head console table at Harewood (fig. 9), attributed to Thomas Chippendale *c*. 1772–5, may be inspired by the Adam tables, but was not designed by Adam.

9. CONSOLE TABLE. Harewood House, Yorkshire. The Gallery.
H: 80.6cm; W: 157.5cm; D: 66.7cm. Carved and gilt wood with semi-circular top of inlaid satinwood. Attributed to Thomas Chippendale who was responsible for most of the furniture at Harewood, *c*. 1772–5.
Although possibly inspired by Adam's table for Sir Laurence Dundas (fig. 8), its composition has a peculiar openness foreign to Adam's style.

10. SIDE TABLE. Syon House, Middlesex. Drawing Room.
H: 81.3cm; W: 180.9cm; D: 88.9cm. Carved and gilt wood with a rectangular mosaic top and reeded brass mounts. One of a pair beneath the pier glasses fig. 53. The tables were not altered, as Bolton presumed (COUNTRY LIFE, 20 December 1919, p.842), from the design (Soane Vol. 17, No. 4) inscribed for the Drawing Room at Syon, and dated 1765. That design was faithfully executed for Croome Court (fig. 11), and the Syon tables were made from an entirely different drawing. Their design, although not preserved in the Soane, is illustrated in the third volume of Adam's *Works* (Plate XI) compiled in 1822 by the publishers, Priestly and Weale, from existing material unused in the previous volumes. It is an error presumably of the publishers (or perhaps of the original engraver, hence Adam's rejection of the plate) that the table and mirror are labelled 'Drawing Room glass and table frame designed for the Earl of Bute.' Except for the pendant festoons, which may have been destroyed or rejected, and the paw feet, the published design is identical to the tables at Syon. The slabs of Roman mosaic, said to have been brought from the Baths of Titus, are recorded in the Syon House Book of 1769 as having cost £200.

11. SIDE TABLE. Philadelphia Museum of Art.
H: 91cm; W: 214cm; D: 87cm. Yellow pine painted white with rectangular green marble top. One of a pair formerly in the piers of the Long Gallery at Croome Court. Executed from a design dated 1765 for a 'Table frame for the Drawing Room at Sion' (Soane Vol.

17, No. 4). The pendant anthemion and festoons indicated in the drawing were either rejected or have been lost. Kentian motifs like the masks are here fully assimilated into a distinctly classicizing composition. The mirror behind is presumably also by Adam, although no design is known. The present whereabouts of the mirror is unknown.

12. SIDE TABLE. Syon House, Middlesex. Vestibule.
H: 84.5cm; W: 181.6cm; D: 92.1cm. Carved and gilt wood with rectangular mosaic top. One of three, the second of the same size with a pink veined marble top, and the third smaller with a green marble top. Executed with modifications from a design for a 'Table frame for the Dining Room at Sion' dated 1765 (Soane Vol. 17, No. 3). While the legs have been slightly simplified, the frieze has been made more ornate by the use of a fluted rather than a plain ground to which the alternating urns and anthemion are applied. The table designed for the Vestibule in 1765 (Soane Vol. 17, Nos. 1, 2), and published in *The Works,* Volume III, Plate XI (fig. B) as a Drawing Room table for the Earl of Bute was either greatly altered or not executed as no piece of that description is known at Syon.

13. SIDE TABLE. Syon House, Middlesex. Entrance Hall.
H: 92.1cm; W:220.9cm; D: 102.2cm. Carved wood painted off-white with rectangular inlaid marble top. Although there is no design for this table, it is most probably by Adam, and of the same date as the Vestibule tables (fig. 12), which have similar legs and the same heaviness of form typical of the

Adam style in the mid-60s. The size of the table is certainly not adapted to its present position in front of the Dying Gaul. It may well have been intended for a different place in the Hall as it is exceedingly difficult to imagine such a large piece in any other room at Syon.

14. 'DESIGN OF A TABLE FRAME FOR THE EARL OF COVENTRY.' Sir John Soane's Museum. Vol. 17, No. 10.
Pen and ink and water-colour. H: 29cm; W: 40.5cm. Inscribed with title and dated Aug. 1767. Adam's experiments with this type of highly complex and varied leg, here with a block capital, a rectangular panel of double guilloche, and a turned, tapered, and fluted shaft with lotus capital and ball foot, is limited to the years 1767–8 during which it appears several times always in different form (figs. 15,16,38). It constitutes something of a transitional type between the rather heavy and rigid legs of his first designs and the slender ones of the 1770s. This is also the period in which Adam begins to use urns as decorative enrichments worked into the stretcher, a practice already known in earlier English and French furniture.

15. SIDEBOARD TABLE. Osterley Park, Middlesex. Dining Room.
H: 86.4cm; W: 213.4cm; D: 91.4cm. Carved and gilt wood. The top mahogany with recessed borders of carved ornament gilded to imitate metal mounts. Executed from a design at Osterley, dated 1767, and published, with the accompanying urns and pedestals (fig. 132), and a wine cooler (not known to exist), in *The Works,* Volume III (Plate IX), erroneously labelled as from Syon House. *En*

suite with two smaller and somewhat simpler pier tables, the legs with lotus capitals and no blocks above, and the friezes without pendant anthemion; both with mosaic tops.

16. CONSOLE TABLE. Bowood, Wiltshire. H: 90.2cm; W: 171.5cm; D: 67.9cm. Carved wood painted white with semi-circular green marble top. Formerly at Lansdowne House. Executed from a design dated 1768 (Soane Vol. 17, No. 15; finished version at Bowood) and inscribed for 'the Room between Anti Room and Library in the 1 pair of stairs at Shelburne House.' One of the simplest, and perhaps latest versions of the turned leg with lotus capital employed by Adam *c*. 1767–8.

17. 'TABLE FRAME FOR THE EARL OF SHELBURNE.' Sir John Soane's Museum. Vol. 17, No. 13.
Pen and ink. H: 12.5cm; W: 27.8cm. Inscribed with title and dated July 1768. The unusual curvilinear shape and scrolled foliate members have no specific precedent in earlier furniture designs, but do bear comparison with some of the tables in Piranesi's *Diverse maniere d'adornare i camini,* 1769. The intricacy and lightness of the forms may have come to both artists through antique bronze objects. There is a rough sketch (Soane Vol. 3, No. 40) showing the table with a mirror (fig. 85) above it.

18. 'GLASS AND TABLE FRAME FOR THE ANTI ROOM AT SHELBURNE HOUSE.' Sir John Soane's Museum. Vol. 20, No. 26.
Pen and ink. H: 49.2cm; W: 15.9cm. Inscribed with title and dated 1768. The measurements of the glass given—8ft. 11in. x 3ft. 11½in. Both pieces executed by John Gilbert and recorded in his bill for carving done at Lansdowne House from 1767 to 1768: 'Ante Room. To making Carving and Gilding in Burnished Gold a large Glass frame with ornaments at top and bottom £33; To making Carving and gilding in Burnished Gold a Circular table frame under ditto, full enriched £30.' (Bolton, II, p.345.) On the reverse of Adam's bill of charges, delivered 21 August 1769 (listing the designs for the table £3 3s. and for the glass frame £2 2s.), are some observations by Lord Shelburne including a complaint that 'The Glass frame in the Anti Room is very ill executed & Wants Gilding again.' (Bolton, II, p.341.) The whereabouts of the pieces are unknown. They were probably sold with the rest of the Lansdowne House furniture in 1806. The table is especially interesting for its relationship to the ram's head console designed in 1765 for Arlington Street (fig. 8). A comparison of the two pieces perfectly illustrates the course and rapidity of Adam's stylistic development. The remarkably thin curved or cabrioled supports employed in this and the preceding design (fig. 17) appear to be purely experimental. Not only do they depart from other Adam designs of the period, notably the Lansdowne House stools also of 1768 (fig. 111), but they are not repeated in his later work. A design for an almost identical mirror was made for Lord Coventry's in Piccadilly, 1768 (Soane Vol. 20, No. 63).

19. SIDEBOARD TABLE. Ellery Sedgwick. H: 87cm; W: 198.1cm; D: 84.7cm. Height of rail: 38.1cm. Carved pine painted white. One of a pair from Kenwood. Although no

design is known, the table with its pedestals, urns, and other accompaniments (fig. a) is illustrated in *The Works* (Vol. I, No. 2, 1774, Plate VIII.) It was probably executed *c*. 1768–9 by William France, and may be identified with the '. . . 2 very rich frames for your Tables with 8 legs to Each richly carv'd ye ornaments under the rails finished in a Masterly manner & mouldings also & sweep'd stretching rails glued up 4 times ye whole carved with the greatest accuracy and gilded in Burnish'd gold in the most perfect manner . . . £33 16s. each, £67 12s.' included in his bill (receipted March 1770) for works made to Adam's design. The white paint would therefore be later. The pair to this table, lacking some of its pendant ornaments, is illustrated with the pedestals and urns in Ralph Edwards, *Dictionary of English Furniture* (Vol. III, fig. 13, p.128). Its owner is unknown.

20. WINE COOLER. The Wernher Collection. Luton Hoo, Bedfordshire.
H: 60.9cm; W: 77.5cm; D: 45.4cm. Carved mahogany with chased ormolu mounts. From the Kenwood sideboard composition (fig. a) illustrated in *The Works* (Vol. I, No. 2, Plate viii). Probably executed by William France *c*. 1770. Alterations from the published design include the substitution of lion for human masks, and round for rectangular feet.

21. SIDE TABLE AND PIER GLASS. Saltram House, Devonshire. Velvet Drawing Room.
TABLE:—H: 87.6cm; W: 105.4cm; D: 55.9cm. Carved and gilt wood with shaped marble top. One of a pair fitted into narrow recesses on either side of the double doors

leading to the Saloon. Executed by Joseph Perfetti (John Parker's account book:—'31st March 1772. To Perfetti for Table Frames in the Velvet Room . . . £41') from a design by Adam inscribed 'Glass and Table Frame for John Parker, Esq.,' and dated 1771 (Soane Vol. 20, No. 70). This design is identical to one for a table without a stretcher, inscribed for the Archbishop of York at Brodsworth, and dated May 1768. The table appears again in a design for Lady Bathurst, undated but *c*. 1778–9 contemporary with other furniture designed for Apsley House.
MIRROR:—H: 212.1cm; with crest 254cm; W: 106.7cm. Carved and gilt wood frame. One of a pair over the tables. The same mirror, with a different crest, appears in a design of 1771 inscribed for John Stewart of Mitcham, Surrey (Soane Vol. 20, No. 80).

22. SIDE TABLE AND MIRROR. Saltram House, Devonshire. The Saloon.
TABLE:—H: 86.4cm; W: 172.7cm; D: 83.8cm. Carved and gilt wood with rectangular inlaid marble top. One of a pair executed 1771 by Joseph Perfetti (John Parker's account book:—'Jan 29, 1771. Pd. Perfetti for Table Frames for the Great Room Saloon . . . £41 1s.'). No design for the table is known. Despite its close relationship to the pieces in the Velvet Drawing Room (fig. 21), its differences suggest an imitation by another hand (possibly Perfetti), rather than a specific design by Adam himself. The festoons instead of being carried around the back of the legs and then down, as they are in the Drawing Room table and in all of Adam's designs, are brought straight across the front leaving an unhappy space at

each corner; the half patera and bucranium, although typical Adam motifs, do not seem to be integrated into the design, but added to it; the feet and capitals are considerably simplified and less elegant; and the geometrical ornament of the frieze is again typical of Adam, but incompatible with the other details.

MIRROR:–H: 266.7cm; with crest 335.3cm; W: 162.5cm. Carved and gilt wood frame. One of four facing each other on the wall and window piers. Executed with alterations from a design (Soane Vol. 20, No. 69) for a 'Glass frame for the Great Drawing Room at Saltram,' dated 1769, which has a slightly different arrangement of the crest figures, and a triton on the base.

The design gives the measurements of the glass as 8ft. x 4ft. 6in.

23. 'FRAME FOR THE ALABASTER TABLES FOR LUTON.' Sir John Soane's Museum. Vol. 17, No. 19.

Pen and ink and water-colour. H:29.5cm; W: 32.8cm. Inscribed with title and dated 17 November 1772. The pairing of the legs to receive a drawer or apron under the frieze is unusual in England at this date, but not uncommon in France particularly for writing tables.

The device also appears on a table of similar design illustrated in *The Works* (Vol. I, No. 1, 1773, Plate VIII), and described by Adam as a 'commode table . . . executed for us in gilt wood' (fig. 150). In addition, there is an undated sketch (Soane Vol. 6, No. 129) enigmatically entitled 'The Antique Tables,' showing a smaller table with a larger frieze, and similarly placed aprons or drawers.

24. SIDE TABLE. Formerly C. F. Kindermann.

Measurements unknown. Carved and gilt wood with a rectangular scagliola top. From 20 St. James's Square. Executed from a design (Soane Vol. 17, No. 22) inscribed '. . . Frame for the Scagliola tables for Sir Watkin Wynne Baronet,' and dated 24 August 1773. The close pairing of the legs, and the sophisticated smoothness of the ornament are characteristic of Adam's fully developed style.

25. SIDEBOARD, PEDESTALS, AND URNS. National Museum of Wales.

TABLE:—H: 91.4cm; W: 274.3cm; D: 106cm. Carved wood painted pale green with pale blue and white details. Formerly in the Eating Room at 20 St. James's Square. Executed from a design (Soane Vol. 17, No. 21) inscribed 'Sideboard table for the Eating Room for Sir Watkin Wynne Bart of Mahogany,' and dated 14 September 1773. There is no design for the pedestals, but they are not unlike those of *c.* 1769 for Kenwood (fig. a).

26. SIDE TABLE. Osterley Park, Middlesex. Tapestry Room.

H: 88.9cm; W: 167.6cm; D: 71.1cm. Carved and gilt wood with semi-circular inlaid marble top (fig. 27). The frieze ornamented with the same rosette and guilloche pattern used on the mirror frame (fig. 8), and overlaid with painted tablets: the centre one of a muse with a lyre (possibly Terpsichore, the Muse of Dancing), and the sides of putti with pipes and tambourine. Executed to a design (Soane Vol. 17, No. 8) inscribed 'Table Frame and Slab for the Tapestry Room at Osterley,' and dated 18 March 1775.

27. TABLE TOP. Osterley Park, Middlesex. Tapestry Room.

White marble inlaid with pale pink, blue, violet, and yellow scagliola. The outer anthemion border repeated in the same colours (violet and white) in the ceiling. The colour and composition are noticeably weak in comparison with the surrounding Gobelins tapestries. Simplified from a design (Soane Vol. 17, No. 8) dated 1775.

28. PIER TABLE. Nostell Priory, Yorkshire. The Hall.

H: 97.8cm; W: 158.7cm; D: 72.4cm. Carved and gilt wood with a rectangular coloured marble top. One of a pair executed with slight modifications, mainly in the frieze, from a design (Soane Vol. 17, No. 28) inscribed '. . . two tables for the Hall to have Statuary slabs at Nostel,' and dated 10 June 1775.

29. PIER TABLE. Nostell Priory, Yorkshire. The Saloon.

H: 93.9cm; W: 144.7cm; D:63.5cm. Carved and gilt wood with semi-circular inlaid scagliola top (fig. 30) supported by square tapered legs with oval medallions of female figures, and square Composite capitals. The shaped stretcher fitted in the centre with a low pedestal and putti supporting an urn, the base of which is missing. One of a pair executed from a design (Soane Vol. 17, No. 28) inscribed 'Plan and elevation of two tables for the Salon the tops to be of Scagliola,' and dated 10 June 1775. The fluted frieze shown in the design was used on the Hall tables (fig. 28), and the anthemion frieze on the design for the latter was used on this pair in the Saloon.

30. SCAGLIOLA TABLE TOP. Nostell Priory. Yorkshire. The Saloon.

Executed by the firm of Richter and Bartoli whose invoice 28 February 1777 records that the tops were made 'According to Mr. Adam's desaign [sic] for Nostell.' The design (Soane Vol. 49, No. 42) is inscribed 'For Sir Rowland Winn slabs for the Salon at Nostell,' and dated 12 August 1775.

31. TABLE TO SUPPORT A CASKET OR BOX. Sir John Soane's Museum. Vol. 17, No. 33.

Pen and ink and water-colour. H: 51.9cm; W: 35.1cm. Inscribed 'For George Keate, Esq.,' and dated 1777. The table rendered with alternate colour schemes: left—gold and white ornament on a black ground, the frieze pink with black and gold tablet; right—terracotta ground with gold ornament, and black and gold tablet. Both schemes are representative of the Etruscan style. The box outlined above was probably to contain part of George Keate's notable collection of coins, shells, or other antique or natural objects. Mrs. Delany on visiting the Keates in 1779 comments that she was 'much entertained in their museum.' (*The Autobiography and Correspondence of Mary Granville, Mrs. Delany*. Vol. II, second series. 1862. p.433.)

32. SIDE TABLE. Osterley Park, Middlesex. Breakfast Room.

H: 83.8cm; W: 111.8cm; D: 67.3cm. Carved and gilt wood with rectangular marble top. One of a pair forming a wall composition with the mirrors (fig. 74) executed from a design (Soane Vol. 20, No. 49) dated 24 April 1777. The over simplified and delicate form lacking in vitality is characteristic of Adam's late work.

33. 'DESIGN OF A TABLE FRAME AND TOP FOR LADY BATHURST'S DRESSING ROOM.' Sir John Soane's Museum. Vol. 17, No. 48.

Pen and ink and water-colour. H: 37cm; W: 29.6cm. Inscribed with title and dated 19 June 1779. The frame to be gilt with painted medallions, and the top to be painted or inlaid with light blue, green, and pink ornaments on a white ground. The figured plaques are a favourite ornamental device of late Adam designs. Note the extremely simplified decoration of the top and streamlining of the legs.

34. 'SIDEBOARD FOR THE DUKE OF CUMBERLAND.' Sir John Soane's Museum. Vol. 17, No. 57.

Pen and ink and water-colour. H: 34.7cm; W: 62.9cm. Inscribed with title and dated 28 October 1780. An unusually large sideboard (measurements given in pencil as 10ft. long) of simple form, painted terracotta, black, and white in the Etruscan style. The urns and pedestals are almost identical to ones designed c. 1780 for Sir John Ramsden at Byram, Yorks. (Soane Vol. 25, No. 156). The figured frieze and tablets with terracotta and white figures on a black ground imitating Etruscan vases.

Adam's designs for altering, enlarging, and redecorating Cumberland House formerly York House, now destroyed), Pall Mall, for H.R.H. Frederick Duke of Cumberland date between 1780 and 1788.

His furniture designs are not known to have been executed.

35. SIDEBOARD TABLE. Saltram House, Devonshire. Dining Room.

H: 90.2cm; W: of each of the three sides 210.8cm; W: across the bay 510.5cm; D: in centre 80cm. Carved wood painted cream with green and white ornament matching the surrounding wall and ceiling decorations. The top mahogany with gilt brass mounts. The table is composed of three separate parts joined to make a single unit, and fitted into the bay, the side windows of which were blocked by Adam, and made into niches to receive his imitation Etruscan vases made of composition. Although no design for the table is known, it is contemporary with the accompanying urns and pedestals designed in 1780 (fig. 142). The extreme, and rather dry simplicity of the pieces is typical of the late Adam style.

36. SIDE TABLE AND MIRROR. Saltram House, Devonshire. Dining Room.

TABLE:—H: 83.8cm; W: 182.8cm; D: 83.8cm. Carved wood painted pale green with cream coloured ornament. The rectangular top of grey marble veined with pink. *En suite* with the sideboard, pedestals, and urns (figs. 35,142). The swags and patera repeated in the frieze above the mirror. No design for the table is known.

MIRROR—H: 246.4cm; with crest 284.5cm; W: 175.3cm. Carved wood frame painted white. The crest with a figure medallion painted either by Angelica Kauffmann or by her husband, Antonio Zucchi, who on 27 June 1781 was paid £150 '. . . for Paintings in the Eating Room.' (John Parker's account book.) The mirror may be the one referred to in John Parker's accounts 'June 15, 1781 To Crighton for a Looking Glass . . . £40.'

Executed from a design (Soane Vol. 20, No. 235) dated 5 April 1781. A comparison with the Velvet Drawing Room mirror 1771 (fig. 21), in which the same motifs—sphinxes and medallions—are employed in the crest, illustrates the progress from a naturalistic and somewhat ornate style, closer in spirit to the antique sources, to a highly simplified or abstracted one.

CABINETS AND COMMODES

37. CLOTHES PRESS. Formerly The Earl of Craven, Coombe Abbey, Warwickshire. H: 266.7cm; W: 182.9cm. Carved mahogany. One of a pair sold at Christies 11 April 1923 (lot 68). Except for the base and entablature, the piece is identical to the central portion of a design for a wardrobe of three bays and four upright pilasters for the Earl of Coventry, dated 2 October 1764. (Soane Vol. 17, Nos. 212,213.) Adam's bill to Lord Coventry, 6 May 1767 'To a design for altering the great cloathes press £1 1s.,' may refer to the division of the larger cabinet into two smaller ones like this pair. The partitioning of the decoration, and its rendering in high relief and naturalistic detail are typical of Adam's earliest efforts.

38. BOOKCASE. Metropolitan Museum of Art, New York.
H: 242.6cm; W: 189.2 cm; D: 44.8cm. Pine stained to imitate mahogany with carved and gilt ornament. From Combe Bank, Kent. Executed to a design (Soane Vol. 17, No. 215) dated 1767, and inscribed '. . . for the Right Honourable Lord Frederick Campbell.' The design is essentially a simplified and refined version of the typical Georgian bookcase with the addition of classicizing ornaments. It is similar in detail to a smaller cabinet for Lord Frederick Campbell, also dated 1767 (fig. 57).

39. 'CABINET FOR ROBERT CHILD, ESQ.' Sir John Soane's Museum. Vol. 17, No. 217.
Pen and ink. H: 40.3cm; W: 28.9 cm. Inscribed with title and dated Sept. 1768. Probably for Robert Child's house in Berkeley Square, and to be used for the display of china or other objects. Not known to have been executed. The half finished composition was presumably to be completed by one of the many draughtsmen in Adam's employ. This kind of unfinished design occurs frequently in the Soane collection of Adam drawings, and is illustrative of what was probably the main office procedure.

40. 'CABINETS FOR THE ROOM OVER THE ANTE-ROOM AT SHELBURNE HOUSE.' Sir John Soane's Museum. Vol. 17, No. 216 (Box 3).
Pen and ink and water-colour. H: 35.6cm; W: 61.6cm. Detail. Inscribed with title and dated March 1770. One of a pair of cabinets on either side of a door. An ambitious architectural composition ornamented with a wide range of classical motifs, and accompanied by a collection of urns, presumably of china, coloured white with pink and blue patterns. The design is much more advanced stylistically than the piece designed for Robert Child only two years earlier (fig. 39). The cabinets are not known to have been executed. They seem to have been an after-thought on the part of Lord or Lady Shelburne as Adam's

final bill of charges was submitted in August 1769.

41. CABINET. Victoria and Albert Museum. H: 188.6cm; W: 188.9cm; D: 33.9cm. Rosewood and satinwood veneer with inlaid decoration and gilt bronze mounts framing coloured marble pilasters and eleven *pietre dure* panels of Italian landscape, one of which bears the name of the maker, 'Baccio Capelli Fecit anno 1709 Fiorenze.' From Kimbolton Castle, Huntingdonshire, a Vanbrugh house altered by Adam *c.* 1765 to 1776. Executed with alterations from a design (Soane Vol. 17, No. 218) inscribed 'For the Duchess of Manchester,' and dated 1 June 1771. The original intention was for a larger and more elaborate piece having an arcaded stand, and a higher entablature with female terms above the pilasters. The cabinet has no practical function, but was designed solely for the display of the *pietre dure* panels; hence its shallowness and splayed sides.

42. 'BOOKCASE FOR SIR GEORGE COLEBROOKE BART.' Sir John Soane's Museum. Vol. 17, No. 219 (Box 4).
Pen and ink and water-colour. H: 53.3cm; W: 36.8cm. Inscribed with title and dated 1771. A combined bookcase and desk fitted in a recess between two windows. The entire piece coloured white with gold ornament. The furniture designed for Sir George Colebrooke's house in Arlington Street (figs. 43, 87,113) was probably not executed as in 1773 Sir George went bankrupt. Although the bookcase is entirely English in form and detail, it has something of a French flavour owing perhaps to its gold and white colour and slender proportions.

43. 'DESIGN OF A COMMODE FOR SIR GEORGE COLEBROOKE BART.' Sir John Soane's Museum. Vol. 17, No. 17.
Pen and ink and water-colour. H: 22cm; W: 33.2cm. Inscribed with title and dated 1771. Adam's first full scale use of painted grotesques as furniture decoration. The commode painted white, and the recessed panels blue and green with pink figures. The rams' head capitals, the frames to the pilasters and panels, and the upper moulding of the frieze presumably to be mounted in ormulu or gilt metal. Unlike Adam's later designs, the composition is still segmented, and the ornament relatively large and unrefined. The rectangular shape is soon abandoned for the more elegant semi-circular commode.

44. 'COMMODE FOR HIS GRACE THE DUKE OF BOLTON.' Sir John Soane's Museum. Vol. 17, No. 18.
Pen and ink and water-colour. H: 48.3cm; W: 44.5cm. Detail excluding an ink drawing of the semi-circular top. Inscribed with title and dated January 1773. This is Adam's earliest design for a semi-circular commode. It is also his first commode on which the decoration is applied to the whole of the panels instead of being contained in framed compartments as in the 1771 commode for Sir George Colebrooke (fig. 43). The piece was intended for Bolton House, Russell Square.

45. COMMODE. Osterley Park, Middlesex. Drawing Room.
H: 91.4cm; W: 152.4cm; D: 60.9cm. Veneered with hardwood, the frieze of satinwood, the whole inlaid with various woods, and mounted with chased and fire gilt brass

mouldings and other ornaments. One of a pair under the pier glasses (fig. 65), executed *c*. 1773. The central medallion of Venus and Cupid (Diana and her hounds in the pair) inlaid in light woods on a dark ground. The flanking candelabra also inlaid with the portrait and figure medallions stained green. The side panels of both commodes with nymphs in oval frames. The frieze, of acanthus and urns overlaid with a tablet of winged griffons and portrait medallions in gilt brass, repeats the frieze over each of the four doors to the room. Although there are no designs for the entire commode, there are a few for the parts: one (Soane Vol. 18, No. 63) for the 'Top of Commode for Robert Child Esq.' dated 30 January 1773, and coloured for painting rather than inlay as executed; three others undated (Soane Vol. 25, No. 210 and Vol. 5, Nos. 20,21) for ornaments of the side panels, one of these (Soane Vol. 5, No. 20) as executed. The maker is unknown, but the superb craftsmanship may be compared with that of the Library suite possibly by John Linnell (fig. 109). These are the only documented Adam commodes known to exist, and are among the finest pieces executed to his design.

46. COMMODE. Osterley Park, Middlesex. Bedroom.

H: 91.4cm; W: 152.4cm; D: 60.9cm. Carved and gilt wood with black and gilt lacquer panels, and top. The frieze and base mouldings, the ornamented pilasters and rams' head capitals all painted to imitate gilt metal mounts. The central frieze opens as a single drawer, and the panel below as one large door. Whether Adam is responsible for the entire commode is conjectural as there are

no designs. The classicizing frame, however, would appear to be his work. There is another Japan commode with a slightly serpentined front and similar mounts with lions' instead of rams' heads, formerly in the Etruscan Room at Osterley, and now in the Victoria and Albert Museum.

47. 'FRONT (AND TOP) OF A COMMODE IN THE COUNTESS OF DERBY'S DRESSING ROOM.' *The Works in Architecture of Robert and James Adam*. Vol. II, No. 1. 1779. Plate VIII.

Engraved by B. Pastorini. H: 58.5cm; W: 44cm. Detail from a plate published 1777, signed Robert Adam 1774, and described in the text as '. . . parts at large of the Finishing and furniture of the Earl of Derby's house . . .'. The original design (Soane Vol. 17, No. 24), dated 21 October 1774, is one of the earliest for furniture in the so-called 'Etruscan' style, characterized by its colour, here terracotta and black on a pale blue ground. The uppermost mouldings, the rams' head capitals, and the narrow borders framing the frieze and the pilasters to be mounted in gilt metal.

48. 'DESIGN OF A BOOKCASE FOR LADY WYNNE'S DRESSING ROOM.' Sir John Soane's Museum. Vol. 17, No. 222.

Pen and ink and water-colour. H: 40.3cm; W: 23.8cm. Inscribed with title and dated 9 February 1776. The finished version of a rough ink sketch (Soane Vol. 23, No. 239). One of a pair of cabinet-bookcases executed by Richard Collins with paintings by Antonio Zucchi. Sir Watkin Williams Wynne's record of expenses for 20 St. James's Square includes a payment of £15 18s. 7¼d. on 12

July 1776 to Richard Collins, carpenter and Clerk of Works, 'for two Bookcases executed to a design of Messrs. Robert and James Adam (mahogany).' (Wynnstay Mss. National Library of Wales, Aberystwyth). The work described in detail in Collins' bill corresponds exactly with this design. Zucchi's bill of 8 June 1776 'To ornamenting 4 Tablets &c in Bookcases for Lady Wynne's dressing room £20' is receipted 15 June 1776 with the comment 'I do promise to retouch the 2 Bookcases & finish them to the satisfaction of Mr. Adam.' The drawer under the ornamented doors suggests that the piece served as a combined bookcase-writing desk. The cabinet form appears to have been chosen as more appropriate to a lady's dressing room than the normal type of bookcase for which designs had in fact been prepared only two days earlier (Soane Vol. 17, Nos. 220,221). These, inscribed 'Lady Wynne's Bookcase' and dated 7 February 1776, show a full length case with open shelves divided into three sections by female terms.

49. 'COMMODE FOR THE SECOND DRAWING ROOM AT APSLEY HOUSE.' Sir John Soane's Museum. Vol. 17, No. 43. Pen and ink and water-colour. H: 34.3cm; W: 44.5cm. Inscribed with title and dated June 1779. A finished and coloured version of a design dated 1777 in the Victoria and Albert Museum (E 3225–1938). There is also an unfinished drawing in the Soane dated 29 October 1778 (Soane Vol. 17, No. 35). A comparison with the Earl of Derby's commode 1774 (fig. 47) reveals a similarity in the kind of ornament particularly on the frieze and pilasters, but a notable decrease in its quantity, and a simplification of its form.

The result is a more elegant and sophisticated design. The commode is coloured cream with pale green ornament. The portrait medallions are red, the figured one blue, and the rosettes pink. The pilasters are dark green, the borders and rams' head capitals gold, presumably to imitate or to be executed in gilded metal.

50. 'GLASS FRAME AND COMMODE FOR SIR JOHN GRIFFIN.' Sir John Soane's Museum. Vol. 20, No. 199. Pen and ink and water-colour. H: 40.5cm; W: 29.1cm. Inscribed with title and dated November 1778. Two individual pieces of furniture combined to form an elaborate decoration for a projecting wall. The caryatids or urns supporting the mirror are presumably two dimensional ornaments applied to the wall. The commode, more accurately described as a chest of drawers with side cupboards, is painted cream with pink, blue, and green grotesque panels and gilt mounts. The mirror frame is gilt, and the wall behind pale lavender-pink. For Sir John Griffin's house in New Burlington Street for which Adam made designs 1778–9. Fragmentary bills for 'Carpenters and Joiners work done by Messrs. Hoberast examined and settled by Robert and James Adam, 18 March 1779' are in the Essex Record Office. They include moving, mending, and fitting up furniture, but give no description of the pieces.

51. 'GLASS AND COMMODE FOR GEORGE KEATE ESQ.' Sir John Soane's Museum. Vol. 20, No. 110. Pen and ink and water-colour. H: 44.5cm; W: 25.1cm. Inscribed with title and dated 1778. This finished design is preceded by a

slightly different one (Soane Vol. 20, No. 109), also dated 1778 depicting a less austere, tripartite mirror with term divisions and a raised central arch formed of husks ending in a circular crest. The commode painted pale green with white pilasters and darker green ornament. The cold simplicity of the design is a marked contrast to the elaborate glass and commode of the same date for Sir John Griffin Griffin (fig. 50).

MIRRORS

52. MIRROR 'FOR THE DRAWING ROOM AT THE EARL OF THANETS IN GROSR. SQUARE.' Sir John Soane's Museum. Vol. 20, No. 3.

Pen and ink and water-colour. H: 43.8cm; W: 26.3cm. Inscribed with title, signed 'Jas Adam Archt,' and dated 1764. One of the earliest efforts by James Adam following his return from Italy in 1763, and the only design for furniture bearing his signature, although others in the Soane may be in his hand. His style shows no appreciable differences from that of Robert Adam. The large scale and quantity of ornament, and the general lack of restraint are characteristic of early Adam mirrors. The mitred-corner frame is a familiar early Georgian type, but the addition of a wide and differently ornamented base is an uncommon, and not entirely satisfactory, choice. The design as a whole is spotty and poorly integrated.

53. PIER GLASS. Syon House, Middlesex. Drawing Room.

W: of glass 165.1cm. Carved and gilt wood frame. One of a pair over the side tables (fig. 10). Identical to a design (Soane Vol. 20, No. 12) inscribed '. . . for a glass of 8 feet 8 Ins by 5 feet for Sir Laurence Dundass,' signed and dated 1765. This design was apparently rejected by Dundas for a very similar one (Soane Vol. 20, No. 11) for a glass '8 feet 9¼ Ins by 4 feet 8¾ Ins . . .', described in Adam's bill of charges for 19 Arlington Street (Bolton II, p.345) as '. . . another Design for the Long Room £5 5 0.' Here, and for at least the next five years, Adam regards the mirror as an independent object clearly separated from the table below.

54. PIER GLASS. Syon House, Middlesex. Dining Room.

W: 131.4cm. Carved and gilt wood frame. One of a pair executed from a design (Soane Vol. 20, No. 14) inscribed '. . . for the Dining Room at Sion House,' and dated 1765 with the width of the glass given as 3ft. 4in. An almost identical design was prepared at the same date for Sir Laurence Dundas (Soane Vol. 20, No. 13). This is probably the '. . . frame for Sir Laurence Dressing Room £3 3s.' listed in Adam's bill of charges for Arlington Street. (Bolton II, p.345.) The design was used again in 1766 for John Luke Niccol (Soane Vol. 20, No. 29). It was published in *The Works,* Vol. III (Plate XI) with other pieces of Syon furniture as the Drawing Room glass for the Earl of Bute at Luton.

55. PIER GLASS. Corsham Court, Wiltshire. Picture Gallery.

H: 381cm. (236.2cm. without decoration): W: 186.7cm. (143.5cm without decoration). Carved and gilt wood frame. One of four executed with minor alterations from design in the Soane and at Corsham. The unfinished Soane design (Vol. 20, No. 55) dated 1767, and the completed copy at Corsham show the mirror with a similar but much less elaborate crest, a tracery border, side festoons, and sphinxes on small plinths at the lower corners, their tails of scrolled acanthus forming an apron across the base. The other Corsham drawing, undated and uninscribed, is for a mitred-corner frame without an inner border. It does, however, show the apron with sphinxes, no plinths, and simpler acanthus scrolls as executed. The final piece is thus a combination of the two Corsham designs with an enlarged crest. The sphinxes are an unusual addition, and reappear only in a design for a mirror for Lansdowne House 1768 (Soane Vol. 20, No. 25). There are no designs for the table the details of which are peculiarly unlike Adam.

56. PIER GLASS. Osterley Park, Middlesex. Long Gallery.
H: 365.8cm; W: 137.2cm. Carved and gilt wood frame. One of four on alternate piers. Except for the absence of festoons suspended from the acanthus scrolls at the base, the mirrors are identical to a design (Soane Vol. 20, No. 23 Box 1) inscribed for the Earl of Shelburne and dated 1768. This design bears a faint pencil inscription 'Glass frame . . . . for Osterley' and the measurements of the glass 6ft. 6in. x 3ft. 3in. An exact copy was formerly at Osterley (present location unknown, N.B.R. photograph 1947).

57. DESIGN FOR A MIRROR AND CABINET. Sir John Soane's Museum. Vol. 20, No. 31.
Pen and ink. H: 44.8cm; W: 29cm. In-scribed 'For Lord Frederick Campbell,' and dated 1767. Adam's first combination of two pieces of furniture forming a single continuous unit. The idea of bringing the mirror down to the top of the cabinet is probably derived from France. Not only has it no precedent in England, but it is also exceptional in Adam's work of this date. Until the early 1770s the pier glass (as opposed to the overmantel mirror) remains a purely independent article usually with an apron separating it from the table below. Here the urn applied to the glass makes the transition between the two objects, and visually enhances their relationship. This also appears to be one of Adam's first mirrors with a medallion crest, another device already known in France, and frequently employed by Neufforge. The fact that the measurements of the glass, normally imported from France, are given in French as well as English inches suggests that the piece was executed. The cabinet is related in its severe masculine shape and simple decoration to the bookcase for Lord Campbell (fig. 38). These, as far as we know, are Adam's only furniture designs for Combe Bank, Kent, an earlier house by Roger Morris to which Adam made additions c. 1775–7. Lord Frederick Campbell, third son of the 4th Duke of Argyll, was Privy Counsellor and Lord Register of Scotland.

58. PIER GLASS, Kenwood, Middlesex. Library.
H: 228.6cm; W: 106.7cm. Carved and gilt wood frame. One of a pair in the window piers designed c. 1767–8 and published in *The Works,* Vol. I, No. II, 1774 (Plate VIII). Samuel Curwen visiting Kenwood in

1776 described the mirrors as 'the largest . . . I ever saw being seven and a half feet high by three and a half in breadth.' (Edwards, *Dictionary of English Furniture,* Vol. II, p.351.) Adam's undated section through the Library (Soane Vol. 14, No. 115) shows the mirrors with painted rather than gilded medallions, a type of applied ornament which becomes one of Adam's favourites. The maker may have been William France who was responsible for other furniture at Kenwood. There is a mirror of similar design but less elongated proportions in Adam's Music Room at Mellerstain in Berwickshire.

59. MIRROR AND SOFA. (Kenwood Library) *The Works in Architecture of Robert and James Adam.* Volume I, No. 2, 1774. Plate V.
Engraved by J. Zucchi. H: 45.5cm; W: 60cm. Detail from a plate entitled 'Section of one of the Sides of the Great Room or Library at Kenwood,' dated 1767. The mirror and sofa were both executed *c.* 1769–70 by Wiliam France. They are described in his bill for articles 'perform'd from Mr. Adams Designs' (undated but receipted by France 30 March 1770) as: '. . . 2 Frames to the Plates of Glass in the two Recesses to Mr. Adams drawing ye upright pillars & angular do all enriched with the most Delicate Antique Ornaments & Arches of light ornaments Issuing from the pillars & a rich freze at top of the whole & bottom ornaments supported from the Base for the Centre of each plate with a Baso Relieve & all the ornaments curiously work'd and the whole gilt in Burnish'd gold & plate Brass behind all the Centre ornaments to keep square. £149 8s. ... 2 Sophas made to Mr.

Adams Design carv'd & gilt in burnish'd Gold the carving all finished in very Elaborate manner. £50 14s.' The glass was obtained by agreement from Thomas Chippendale. On 14 July 1769 the latter contracted with Adam to 'deliver in about Two Months to Mr. Adam Architect The Following French Plate Glass in London Silver'd and ready to put up.' When the specified time had elapsed Chippendale presumably requested three months extension and payment on account of half the total bill (£340). Although the agreement had been signed by Adam, its transaction was the responsibility of the chief cabinet-maker, William France. Thus, instead of paying £170 directly to Chippendale or to Adam, Lord Mansfield gave it to France who was not only responsible for handing it over to Chippendale, but was also committed to redeem it from him, or to repay it himself should the order fail to materialize. Fortunately for France the order was completed, and on 29 November the remaining £170 was paid to Thomas Chippendale junior for his father's work as a glass merchant. France then records unpacking the glasses, measuring them for frames, and consulting with Adam on fitting them to the wall. At this point the original plan to have the mirrors flush with the wall (like the bookcases) was scrapped, and it was decided to cut away the recesses. The unusual size of the mirrors, 6½ft. high by 8ft. wide, may account for the change of plan. Adam's undated pencil sketch for the mirror with a stool below (Soane Vol. 3, No. 31) inscribed 'Oak frame first on the wall —?— Plate Glass' does not show the recesses. The coloured section of the side of the room (Soane Vol. 14, No. 114), also undated, shows one mirror set back with a stool beneath, and the other flush with the wall and framed by two projecting pilasters, and with the sofa. This is Adam's first tripartite composition and his earliest use of the mirror as a large scale wall decoration. It is interesting to note that a design (Soane Vol. 40, No. 15) of almost identical description was suggested for Kedleston, the date and proposed location unknown. The executed sofa, except for its legs, is identical to the engraving and to an undated sketch (Soane Vol. 6, No. 151). William France also executed to Adam's design '. . . three Scrole headed Sopha frames for the Windows carved & gilt in burnish'd Gold the carving all done on the same principal as the sophas £48.' The design and present ownership of these pieces is unknown. They were probably the stools depicted in the sketch of the mirror, and section of the room (Soane Vol. 3, No. 31; Vol. 14, No. 114) discussed above.

60. 'GLASS FRAME FOR WILLIAM WEDDELL ESQ AT NEWBY.' Sir John Soane's Museum. Vol. 20, No. 78.
Pen and ink and water-colour. H: 59.3cm; W: 28.5cm. Inscribed with title and dated 1770. One of Adam's few designs for William Weddell who obtained a great deal of his furniture for Newby from France. The exaggerated height of the glass (according to the scale approximately 8ft. x 2ft. 6in.), and the style of the frame, which is closer to Adam's work of *c.* 1765-7 (a period of French influence) than of 1770, may be concessions to Weddell's Gallic tastes.

61. MIRROR. Corsham Court, Wiltshire. Cabinet Room.

H: 323.2cm (without decoration 207.6cm); W: 195.6cm (without decoration 146.1cm). Carved and gilt wood frame. There are two designs in the Soane and one at Corsham. The first Soane design (Vol. 20, No. 57), inscribed 'Glass and Table Frame for the Room next the Great Room at Corsham for Paul Methuen Esq,' and dated 1771, shows a wide fluted frame with mitred corners; a crest of two female figures seated on small acanthus scrolls, and centering an oval medallion framing an urn; draped festoons at the sides; and an apron of smaller festoons with a central mask surmounted by a basket. The inner tracery border does not appear. The table is of simple semi-circular form on four round legs joined by a stretcher with an urn supported by sphinxes worked in. The Corsham design is identical but bears an additional pencil sketch of a shaped pedestal with vase candelabrum, drawn by another hand, and a faint inscription '4 girandoles for the 4 corners of Great Room (the room next to the Cabinet Room). Commode 4½ft. long 3ft. high.' There is an Adam design for a girandole (Soane Vol. 20, No. 58) dated 18 April 1772, and a copy at Corsham. Neither the girandoles nor the table were executed. Although Adam may have intended to provide designs for a commode, none are known. He is certainly not responsible for the design of the splendid inlaid commode and torcheres made by John Cobb 1772. The second Soane design (Vol. 20, No. 56) is dated 6 March 1772 and does not include the table. Here the mirror is depicted with a narrow, straight frame and inner tracery border as executed, but the side festoons are omitted, and a basket is added to the centre of the small festoons at the base. In each of the three designs the crest is simpler and more compact, without the acanthus scrolls surrounding the whole of the oval glass. The final piece can thus be regarded as a combination of the 1771 and 1772 designs with minor alterations. A comparison with the mirror in the Picture Gallery, 1767 (fig. 55) reveals a considerable refinement of the entire composition and its details.

62. MIRROR, TABLE, AND TRIPODS (Luton Park, Bedfordshire) *The Works in Architecture of Robert and James Adam.* Volume III, 1822. Plate VIII.
Engraving H: 46cm; W: 32.5cm. Erroneously entitled 'Furniture at Sion House,' it corresponds to a design (Soane Vol. 20, No. 116) inscribed 'Glass and Table frame and Tripods for the Drawing Room at Luton;' the mirror dated 1 October 1772, and the table and tripods 27 October 1772. This is Adam's first design for a tripartite mirror with raised centre and female terms. The undated sketch (Soane Vol. 3, No. 31) for the mirrors at Kenwood (fig. 59), and the design of 1770 (Soane Vol. 20, No. 38) for an overmantel mirror for Mr. Child, Berkeley Square, are examples of his earlier three bay type divided by tapering pilasters with female busts rather than three-quarter terms.

63. 'GLASS FRAME FOR THE END OF THE DRAWING ROOM AT BOLTON HOUSE.' Sir John Soane's Museum. Vol. 20, No. 84.
Pen and ink and water-colour. H: 41.8cm; W: 32.5cm. Inscribed with title and dated 22 October 1772. The tripartite mirror is conceived in architectural terms with a traceried frieze and pilasters, and a central arch reminiscent of a fanlight. The suggestion of a 'Palladian' window is further enhanced by the balcony-like rail below. The measurements of the glass given: H: rail 7½in.; main glass 80½in.; arched crest 1ft. 7in. (total 8ft. 11in.); W: central bay 40½in.; side bays each 20in. (total 5ft. 0½in.). The designs for other mirrors for the Drawing Room of Bolton House, Russell Square (Soane Vol. 20, Nos. 82,83) are of a similar type.

64. 'DESIGN OF A CHIMNEY PIECE FOR THE DRESSING ROOM AT THE EARL OF HARRINGTON'S.' Sir John Soane's Museum. Vol. 23, No. 15 (Box 4). Pen and ink and water-colour. H: 60.5cm; W: 42.5cm. Inscribed with title. Undated but *c.* 1773 contemporary with another dated design for a Dressing Room mirror (Soane Vol. 20, No. 118) for Lord Harrington's house in St. James's Stable Yard Road (now Clarence Gate). The arched frame with a horizontal division, and the pendant lamps and lunettes are typical of this period (fig. 150). Note the continuation of the wall moulding in the division of the mirror, and the repetition of motifs: the oval medallions in the mirror and chimney piece, and the half patera on the mirror and wall mouldings.

65. PIER GLASS. Osterley Park, Middlesex. Drawing Room.
H: 259.1cm; W: 152.4cm. Carved and gilt wood frame. One of a pair placed above the inlaid commodes (fig. 45). Executed to a design at Osterley dated 21 July 1773. Designs in the Soane (Vol. 20, Nos. 34,35) inscribed 'Glass Frame for the Drawing Room at Osterley,' and dated 1767 were executed for the Dining Room.

66. 'SECTION OF THE DRAWING ROOM NORTHUMBERLAND HOUSE LONDON.' Sir John Soane's Museum. Vol. 39, No. 7.

Pen and ink and water-colour. H: 51cm; W: 65cm. Inscribed with title; undated but c. 1773–4, contemporary with the overmantel mirror (fig. 67). The measurements of the glass with its crest ornament given: H: 10ft. 6¼in.; W: 5ft. 1½in. The walls red, dotted to represent porphyry, and overlaid with gilt ornament; the pilasters and door green with red and gold ornament; the frieze and dado green; the sofa and chair with gilt frames and red and gold upholstery. The design may be related to the one described in Adam's bill to the Duke of Northumberland (in the possession of the Duke of Northumberland, Alnwick Castle) '26 June 1773 To a drawing of the centre pier glass to a large scale £2 12s.' The mirror represents a considerable advance from the Kenwood Library mirror of 1769–70 (fig. 59). Not only are the ornaments much more intricate and refined, but the glass as a whole is now fully assimilated into the wall decoration, and can no longer be considered furniture. The mirror is repeated in the two bays on either side of the chimney piece (Soane Vol. 39, No. 6), and in the three window piers opposite (Soane Vol. 39, No. 5). By virtue of their decoration, the sofa and chair have also become integral parts of the composition. The sofa is similar in form to that designed 20 January 1773 for the Duke of Bolton (fig. 114). French influence noted in the Duke of Bolton's sofa is confirmed by the confident shown in Adam's section of the chimney piece wall of the Northumberland House Drawing Room (Soane Vol. 39, No.

6). This predates the confident of 1780 for Sir Abraham Hume (fig. 124), and appears to be Adam's first design for such a piece. Whether the seat furniture, tables, and commodes illustrated in Adam's sections were executed is not known. The mirrors and wall decorations were carried out with alterations, but only the overmantel mirror (fig. 67) and the first bay (the door and two pilasters) of the two adjacent walls survive.

67. OVERMANTEL MIRROR. Victoria and Albert Museum.

W: 200.6cm. The frame of gilded lead, wood and composition with painted medallion crest. The walls of glass foiled to represent porphyry. From the Glass Drawing Room, Northumberland House (demolished 1874). Adam's bill for Northumberland House (in the possession of the Duke of Northumberland, Alnwick Castle) includes a complete list of his several designs for the mirror: '26 June 1773 To a drawing of the chimney glass for the Drawing Room to a large scale £2 2s. [c.f. Soane Vol. 20, No. 17 similarly dated and inscribed]; 15 March 1774 To another design of a chimney piece and glass for the Drawing Room £8 8s.; 11 April 1774 To a drawing of glass over chimney at full size £2 2s.; 10 May 1774 To making alterations on chimney glass and girandole £1 1s.' A section of the chimney piece wall (Soane Vol. 39, No. 6) shows the overmantel mirror with two full size mirrors on either side, and a confident, and chairs en suite with those in fig. 66. By applying the ornament not only to the mirror but also to the surrounding glass walls, the frame is deprived of its normal function as an enclosure, and the mirror, instead of being an independent object, becomes an integral part of the wall decoration.

68. 'CHIMNEY PIECE FOR THE COUNTESS OF DERBY'S ETRUSCAN DRESSING ROOM OF WHITE MARBLE INLAID WITH SCAGLIOLA IN THE ETRUSCAN TASTE WITH THE GLASS FRAME OVER IT.' *The Works in Architecture of Robert and James Adam.* Volume II, No. 1, 1779. Plate VI.

Engraved by J. Zucchi. H: 44cm; W: 58.5cm. Detail from a plate published 1777, signed and dated Robert Adam architect, 1773. The dating of the plate refers not to the specific piece, but probably to the room. The actual design (Soane Vol. 23, No. 51) is dated 1774 and shows the mirror with its inner frame coloured black with gold ornament; the central frieze pink with red acanthus on a pale blue ground; the crest with a pink and black rosette in a pale blue oval possibly to be glass; and the remaining parts gilt. This design is particularly interesting for its arrangement of overlapping two dimensional forms suggestive of different spatial planes. It is also one of the few mirrors in the so-called 'Etruscan' style indicated here only by the brief use of a black ground.

69. 'GLASS FRAME FOR THE 3RD DRAWING ROOM AT ASHBURNHAM HOUSE.' Sir John Soane's Museum. Vol. 20, No. 142.

Pen and ink and water-colour. H: 44.5cm; W: 29cm. Inscribed with title and dated 25 August 1774. The alignment of classical motifs along a horizontal rod is a new compositional pattern departing from the more common vertical arrangements. It appears only in a few designs of this period. The grotesque, normally a painted ornament, is here intended to be carved, or more likely to be moulded in lead or composition and applied to the wall. The colouring is bright green, purple, and gold. For the Earl of Ashburnham's house No. 19 (now 30) Dover Street. Other designs by Adam for furniture and decoration of Ashburnham House are dated 1773–6.

70. PIER GLASS. Osterley Park, Middlesex. Bedroom.

H: 243.8cm; W: 152.4cm. The frame of carved wood painted green with gilt ornament of moulded composition. The crest of carved and gilt wood with a painted medallion on a glass panel. Executed to a design (Soane Vol. 20, Nos. 46,47) dated 15 May 1775. The green and gold colouring, the sphinxes, putti and other details are repeated in the bed (fig. 128).

71. PIER GLASS. Osterley Park, Middlesex. Etruscan Room.

H: 233.7cm; W: 127cm. The frame of carved wood painted black with gilt ornament of moulded composition. The crest of carved and gilt wood with a painted medallion. Executed to a design (Soane Vol. 20, Nos. 44,45) dated 15 May 1775. Note the extension of the glass into the crest, a new device which seems to have attracted Adam at this moment (fig. 70). As in the overmantel mirror for Derby House (fig. 68), the black colouring is chosen to accord with the Etruscan decorations of the room.

72. 'SECTION OF THE MUSICK ROOM AT LADY HOME'S.' Sir John Soane's

Museum. Vol. 50, No. 34 (Box 4).
Pen and ink and grey wash. H: 44cm; W: 59cm. Detail. Inscribed with title and dated 27 January 1775. The glass cut into an unusual shape at the top (see figs. 70,71) and overlaid with a richly ornamented frame capable of competing with the mirrored piers and other decorations in the room. Unexecuted.

73. 'SECTION OF ONE SIDE OF THE SECOND DRAWING ROOM.' (Derby House, Grosvenor Square) *The Works in Architecture of Robert and James Adam.* Volume II, No. 1, 1779, Plate IV.
Engraved by Josh. Record. H: 58.5cm; W: 44cm. Detail. Identical to the overmantel mirror designed 28 February 1777 (Soane Vol. 23, No. 46) for the opposite wall of the same room and also published in *The Works* (Vol. II, No. 1, Plate III). The mirror explains Walpole's simile 'filigreed into puerility like l'Hotel de Derby.' (H.W. to the Countess of Upper Ossory. 8 August 1777. Toynbee. Vol. X, p.93.) Its lace-like frame is the result of continuous refinements upon the earlier Kenwood mirrors of *c.* 1769 (fig. 59).

74. PIER GLASS. Osterley Park, Middlesex. Breakfast Room.
H: 243.8cm; W: 106.7cm. Carved and gilt wood frame. One of a pair forming a wall composition with the tables (fig. 32), executed from a design (Soane Vol. 20, No. 49) dated 24 April 1777. The small and delicate ornament is much less successful in execution than on paper. For other late designs of mirror and table compositions see figs. 78, 79,80.

75. 'DESIGN OF A GLASS FRAME TO BE PLACED OVER THE CHIMNEY IN LADY BATHURST'S DRESSING ROOM.' Sir John Soane's Museum. Vol. 20, No. 171. (Box 1).
Pen and ink and water-colour. H: 44.7cm; W: 28.8cm. Inscribed with title and dated 31 January 1778. A late and over refined form of the familiar tripartite or 'Palladian' window mirror (figs. 62,63). The measurements of the glass given: H: 7ft. 6in.; W: 4ft. 3in. plus 10in. for each side panel.

76. 'DESIGN OF A GLASS FRAME FOR THE PIERS IN THE GREAT DRAWING ROOM AT BATHURST HOUSE.' Sir John Soane's Museum. Vol. 20, No. 169 (Box 3).
Pen and ink and water-colour. H: 55cm; W: 37.5cm. Inscribed with title and dated 31 January 1778. The measurements of the glass given: 9ft. 5in. x 5ft. 6in. The accompanying pedestals with concave sides, animal feet and rams' head capitals are derived from Roman altars.
The shaft is based upon the well known Vatican candelabrum (fig. 77) which is also on a pedestal ornamented with rams' heads. According to the scale the pedestal candlestands would be full scale pieces of furniture four feet in height.

77. CANDELABRUM. Vatican Museum. Salle dei Candelabri II.
H: 18.5cm (base H: 7.2cm; shaft H: 11.3cm). Marble. Second century, A.D., from S. Costanza, Rome.
The base is triangular in plan. Each of the three sides is ornamented with a putto holding a horn of plenty, sphinxes at the lower corners, and rams' heads above.

78. 'GLASS AND TABLE FRAME FOR THE PIERS IN THE FIRST ROOM AT SIR ABRAHAM HUMES IN HILL STREET.' Sir John Soane's Museum. Vol. 20, No. 202.
Pen and ink and water-colour. H: 42.8cm; W: 16.2cm. Inscribed with title and dated 11 January 1779. The arcaded table is a new form employed by Adam in the late 1770s. The arches are usually limited, however, to the sides or centre (see fig. 80), and are rarely applied to the entire front as they are here. The mirror is also unusual in design, particularly the upper part with an arch in a rectangular frame. The individual motifs are not new. This and the following designs are representative of the late wall compositions of tables and mirrors, which become increasingly feeble with continued refinement.

79. 'PIER GLASS & TABLE FRAME FOR THE GREAT DRAWING ROOM AT SIR ABRAHAM HUMES IN HILL STREET.' Sir John Soane's Museum. Vol. 20, No. 206.
Pen and ink and water-colour. H: 51cm; W: 30.8cm. Inscribed with title and dated 17 March 1779. The most interesting feature of the design is the transition between the table and mirror, formed by a pedestal and urn with projecting candle branches. These forms, although suggestive of actual objects, are two dimensional ornaments applied to the glass. Their projection is shown in the profile sketch to the side. The measurements of the glass given: H: below urn 17in.; above urn 56in. (total 6ft. 1in.); W: 20½in.

80. MIRROR AND TABLE. Sir John Soane's Museum. Vol. 20, No. 216.

Pen and ink and water-colour. H: 47cm; W: 29.6cm. Inscribed 'Duke of Roxburghs 1st Library,' and dated 18 September 1779. The measurements of the glass are given: total height 4ft. 5in. plus 2ft. 11in. (pencil 50½in. plus 35in.); total width 2ft. 9½in. (pencil 31½in. centre; 1ft. sides). The frame was presumably designed for an old glass as the surrounding panels at the sides, top, and base are all inscribed 'New.' This is confirmed by an earlier design, marked 'Unexecuted' (Soane Vol. 20, No. 215), for an arched mirror without the additional surrounds. The table in both designs is painted pale green with gilt ornaments. Note the continuous vertical division through the mirror and table legs, also the repetition of oval medallions in the friezes of both pieces.

81. 'GLASS FRAME FOR THE PIERS IN THE EATING ROOM AT CULLEAN CASTLE.' Sir John Soane's Museum. Vol. 20, No. 228.
Pen and ink and water-colour. H: 45cm; W: 31.2cm. Inscribed with title and dated March 1782. The design was executed in duplicate with slight modifications. The mirrors (recently reassembled with the oval patera in the side panels reversed) are now in the Second or Day Drawing Room at Culzean Castle, Ayrshire. The measurements of the glass included on the drawing: H: centre— 1ft. 1½in. plus 3ft. 2in. plus 1ft. 3in. plus 4in. (total 5ft. 10½in.); sides—1ft. 1½in. plus 3ft. 2in. plus 4in. (total 4ft. 7½in.). W: centre— 1ft. 10¾in.; sides—9½in. each (total 3ft. 5¾in.). Both the design and the executed pieces are of lower quality than most of Adam's earlier furniture. Other designs for mirror frames for the Buffet Room, the Lib-

rary, and the Dressing Room, and a girandole for the Eating Room (Soane Vol. 20, Nos. 231,232,233,236), all dated 1782, were executed, and are preserved at Culzean. Adam's work for Daniel Kennedy, 10th Earl of Cassillis dates from 1778 to 1787.

OVAL MIRRORS AND GIRANDOLES

82. OVAL MIRROR. Kedleston Hall, Derbyshire. Drawing Room.
H: 280cm; W:147cm. Carved and gilt wood frame. One of a pair executed with minor alterations from a design (Soane Vol. 20, No. 8) dated 1765. The drawing calls for two pairs of candle branches, only one of which was executed, and does not include the inner tracery border. The lively acanthus scrolls, although characteristic of Adam mirrors of this date (figs. 52,53), and in keeping with the Baroque flavour of Linnell's Drawing Room sofas (fig. 101), are unexpected in view of the earlier designs for the Kedleston sideboard composition (fig. 3).

83. 'DESIGN OF A GLASS FRAME FOR THE EATING ROOM FOR THE EARL OF COVENTRY.' Sir John Soane's Museum. Vol. 20, No. 66.
Pen and ink and water-colour. H: 58.7cm; W: 23.5cm. Inscribed with title and dated 1768. Probably for Earl of Coventry's house in Piccadilly. The ornamented hanging device is a Rococo invention exploited by Adam as a means of transforming the mirror into a larger wall decoration. The composition is considerably restrained and simplified in comparison with the Kedleston mirror (fig. 82), and other early Adam designs of this type.

84. 'GLASS FRAME FOR LADY COVENTRY'S DRESSING ROOM.' Sir John Soane's Museum. Vol. 20, No. 62.
Pen and ink and water-colour. H: 41.7cm; W: 29.1cm. Inscribed with title and dated 1768. Probably for the Earl of Coventry's house in Piccadilly. The circular glass framed by foliate branches giving way to female terms on the sides, and encircling the Coventry crest above. The eagles, and rocks and foliage below were presumably to be carved in wood or moulded in stucco, and applied to the wall over a dressing table or commode. The design, although it embodies some classical motifs, is essentially Rococo in conception. The latter style was undoubtedly considered most appropriate to the feminine associations of the piece. For other Dressing Room mirrors see figs. 85,86,91.

85. 'GLASS FRAME FOR THE EARL OF SHELBURNE.' Sir John Soane's Museum. Vol. 20, No. 21.
Pen and ink and water-colour. H: 40.2cm; W: 23.9cm. Inscribed with title and dated 1768. The design was probably intended for a Dressing or Bed Room. It was first conceived to be placed over the table (fig. 17) as indicated in the rough sketch (Soane Vol. 3, No. 40). The combination appears to have been rejected, possibly for being too fussy or elaborate. The mirror, however, may well have been executed to another version of this design (Soane Vol. 20, No. 22), with an additional ornamented hanging device and an oval glass of which the measurements are given—5ft. x 3ft. 4in.

86. GIRANDOLE. Osterley Park, Middlesex. Long Gallery.

H: 228.6cm; W: 111.8cm. Carved and gilt wood frame. One of a set of six on the alternate window piers of the Gallery. Executed, probably by John Linnell, with some alterations from Adam's design dated 1770 (Soane Vol. 20, Nos. 36,37). Similar, in shape only, to an earlier design of 1768 for the Earl of Coventry (Soane Vol. 20, No. 61).

87. 'TOILET TABLE FOR LADY COLEBROOKE.' Sir John Soane's Museum. Vol. 17, No. 16.
Pen and ink and water-colour. H: 40.3cm; W: 28.9cm. Inscribed with title and dated 1771. An elaborate arrangement of drapery, table, mirror, urns, and perfume burners. The florid style is specifically adapted for the female patron, and is not typical of Adam's other work of this date. The circular mirror is of the same type as that designed 1768 for Lady Coventry's Dressing Room (fig. 84).

88. 'PIER GLASS IN THE PARLOUR' (Kenwood). *The Works in Architecture of Robert and James Adam.* Vol. I, No. 2, 1774. Plate VIII.
Engraved by P. Begbie. H: 59cm; W: 44cm. Detail. Closest to a design (Soane Vol. 3, No. 46) inscribed 'Oval Glass for the Dining Parlor at Mr. Thynne's,' undated but *c.* 1771–2 contemporary with other designs for The Hon. Fred. Thynne's house in Curzon Street. This design seems to have been rejected by Thynne, for in 1773 it was presented with minor alterations (winged griffons instead of sphinxes on the side projections) to Lord Mansfield. The latter's design (Soane Vol. 20, No. 120) is inscribed 'Glass for the Dining Parlor at Kenwood,

and contains pencil measurements of the glass—3ft. 10in. x 2ft. 8in. Both designs include an ornamented hanging device which is scratched out in the Kenwood version.

89. OVAL MIRROR. Formerly in the possession of Mallett & Son.
Measurements unknown. Carved and gilt wood frame. Identical to the mirror designed for Kenwood 1773, and illustrated in *The Works* (fig. 88). As nothing is known of the history of this piece, it can be presumed that it is either from Kenwood, or is a first-rate copy from *The Works.*

90. 'GLASS FRAME FOR GEORGE KEATE.' Sir John Soane's Museum. Vol. 20, No. 104.
Pen and ink and water-colour. H: 42.7cm; W: 29cm. Inscribed with title and dated 1772. A reworking or amplification of an earlier design with the festoons added, and another name or inscription rubbed out at the base. The measurements of the glass are pencilled in, 2ft. 6in. x 1ft. 10in. The oval mirror with projecting shelves at the sides was first employed *c.* 1771 for The Hon. Frederick Thynne, and repeated in the design for Kenwood 1773 (figs. 88,89).

91. 'GLASS FRAME FOR MR. KEATES DRESSING ROOM.' Sir John Soane's Museum. Vol. 20, No. 106.
Pen and ink and water-colour. H: 45cm; W: 29cm. Inscribed with title and dated 20 October 1772. A comparison with the earlier Dressing Room mirrors of 1768 for Lord Shelburne (fig. 85) and Lady Coventry (fig. 84) illustrates the extent and nature of Adam's refining process. Furniture and in-

teriors for George Keate's house in Charlotte Street (now 10 Bloomsbury Street) were designed by Adam between 1772 and 1778, and were presumably executed.

92. 'PIER GLASS FOR THE ANTI ROOM AT LORD STANLEYS IN GROSVR. SQR.' Sir John Soane's Museum. Vol. 20, No. 133.
Pen and ink and water-colour. H: 43cm; W: 28.9cm. Inscribed with title and dated 27 July 1774. The oval glass is overlaid with concentric borders framing an inner girandole, ornamented in the usual way with sphinxes, rams' heads, urns, and anthemion. The frame and ornaments coloured various shades of green against a pale green wall.

93. 'GIRANDOLE IN THE ETRUSCAN ROOM' (Derby House, Grosvenor Square). *The Works in Architecture of Robert and James Adam.* Volume II, No. 1, 1779. Plate VIII.
Engraved by B. Pastorini. H: 58.5cm; W: 44cm. Detail from a plate published 1777, and signed Robert Adam 1774. Adam's design is not preserved, but must have been *c.* 1774, contemporary with most of the furnishings for The Earl of Derby's house. The various elements—medallions, pendant lamp, urn and candle branches, etc.—linked by chains of husks, form a wall decoration similar to the painted grotesques on the door panels of the room. Copies of *The Works* with selected colour plates (R.I.B.A., B.M., Soane) show the girandole as gilt with black tablets and terracotta figures. The piece was presumably executed for the text describes it, and the related girandoles for the first Drawing Room and Etruscan Room, as 'elegantly carved and gilt, with the painting by Mr. Zucchi.'

94. 'GIRANDOLE FOR THE DRAWING ROOM AT BATHURST HOUSE.' Sir John Soane's Museum. Vol. 20, No. 178.
Pen and ink and water-colour. H: 43.6cm; W: 28.8cm. Inscribed with title and dated 31 January 1778. The girandole worked into a painted wall decoration, the main feature being the central medallion. The sofa outlined below is of notably simple form. Both pieces typify the rather flavourless sophistication of the late Adam style. Adam's designs for the furnishing of Apsley House are not known to have been executed.

95. 'GIRANDOLE FOR LADY BATHURST'S DRESSING ROOM.' Sir John Soane's Museum. Vol. 20, No. 179 (Box 1). Pen and ink and water-colour. H: 43cm; W: 23.7cm. Inscribed with title and dated 31 January 1778. A series of circular and rectangular painted tablets worked into a wall decoration; fitted with candle branches, hence a girandole.

SEAT FURNITURE

96. ARM CHAIR. Alnwick Castle, Northumberland.
H: 161.3cm; W: 51.4cm; D: 63.5cm. Carved wood painted white with gilt detail. Part of Adam's furnishings for the chapel at Alnwick; hence the exceptional use of the Gothic style. The chair corresponds with a design (Soane Vol. 50, No. 21) inscribed 'Copy of one of the Chairs in the Church at Croome for the Earl of Coventry,' and dated

1761. Although it was probably not executed until *c.* 1777–80, the date of Adam's other designs for the Alnwick chapel, in view of its relation to the Croome drawing, it may be considered Adam's first essay in furniture design.

97. DESIGN FOR AN ARM CHAIR by John Linnell. Victoria and Albert Museum (92 D26, E 81–1929).

Pen and ink and water-colour. H: 17cm; W: 15.7cm. Inscribed 'For Sr: Nathl: Curzons.' Although undated, the design must be before 9 April 1761, when Sir Nathaniel Curzon of Kedleston was created Lord Scarsdale. It therefore predates Adam's design of 1762 for a sofa for Lord Scarsdale (fig. 97), presumably intended to be *en suite* with the chair. The many similarities between the two pieces, neither of which was executed for Kedleston, leaves no doubt that Adam knew Linnell's design. While Adam's first efforts as a furniture designer may have been guided by Linnell, Linnell's shift from the Rococo to the Neo-classical style was probably influenced by Adam's designs for a tripod candle-stand, urns, ceilings, and other subjects drawn before 1761, or even by the earlier classicism of James Stuart who preceded Adam at Kedleston. It is more than likely, at least in the early stages of the furnishing of Kedleston, that Adam and Linnell worked hand in hand, Adam profiting from Linnell's experience as a cabinet-maker, and Linnell from Adam's knowledge of antique forms and ornaments.

98. 'DESIGN OF A SOPHA FOR LORD SCARSDALE & ALSO EXECUTED FOR MRS. MONTAGU IN HILL STREET.'

Sir John Soane's Museum. Vol. 17, No. 69. Pen and ink and water-colour. H: 45.5cm; W: 27.5cm. Inscribed with title, signed and dated 'Robert Adam Archt 1762.' While the date can be accepted as contemporary with the drawing, the inscription must be a later addition for Adam surely would not have presented Lord Scarsdale, his first major patron, with a second-hand design blatantly labelled as such. Since no sofa of this description was made for Lord Scarsdale, we can conclude that the design having been rejected by him was then presented to Mrs. Montagu for whom it is said to have been executed. Whether it was executed exactly as it appears in the drawing is unknown for there is no piece to corroborate the inscription. The design does, however, have several features in common with the Philadelphia Museum sofa (fig. 100) for which there is an uninscribed design (fig. 99) not in Adam's hand. The precise relationship between these two sofa designs is unclear. If the anonymous drawing is later than Adam's, then it is obviously influenced by it. If it is earlier, then the Adam design would be a combination of motifs taken from it, and from Linnell's chair (fig. 97). There is reason to believe that the latter is the case. Nevertheless, credit for the mermaids and tritons, the key features of this and of all of the other projects for the Kedleston sofas, must be given to Adam who first introduced the figures in the ceiling (designed 1759) of the Drawing Room for which these pieces were intended.

99. DESIGN FOR A SOFA. Sir John Soane's Museum. Vol. 17, No. 70.

Pen and ink and water-colour. H: 22cm;

W: 35.3cm. No inscription, date, or signature. Possibly another design for Mrs. Montagu's sofa, but almost certainly not by Adam. A comparison with the documented Adam drawing (fig. 98) reveals considerable differences in draughtsmanship especially in the handling of the festoon, the scales, and figures. The shape of the seat rail, the scroll feet, and the ornament on the centre legs strongly suggest a more experienced Rococo designer, possibly John or William Linnell one of whom was employed by Mrs. Montagu as early as 1752. The design is undoubtedly related to Adam's, but whether it was drawn before or after is impossible to determine. The fact that it was executed (fig. 100) with classicizing alterations inspired by Adam's drawing (fig. 98) suggests that it came first. Adam, however, may well have been responsible for the idea of the mermaids, and the medallion crest, a classical motif which also appears on John Linnell's design for a chair (fig. 97) before 1761.

100. SOFA. Philadelphia Museum of Art.
H: 110cm; W: 245cm; D: 119.4cm. Carved and gilt wood, upholstered in modern blue fabric. Executed with modifications from the uninscribed design (fig. 99) possibly for Mrs. Montagu's house in Hill Street. Apart from the cartouches added at the knees, the alterations from the design are entirely of a classical nature: paw feet are substituted for the scrolled ones; the lowered female masks replace the Rococo ornament on the legs; and the drapery held by the mermaids is elongated so as to eliminate the typically Rococo 'C' scrolls which were used to make the transition between the end legs and the seat rail. All of these new features appear in Adam's sofa design (fig. 98) from which they were probably adapted. The piece may therefore be said to represent the combined efforts of Adam and the anonymous designer. The recent history of the sofa is both complicated and amusing. In 1929 it was in the possession of French & Company in New York. It was then purchased by A. G. Lewis, a London dealer, who brought it back to England, restored it, and sold it to the Philadelphia Museum. When it left New York it had a slightly different medallion without the present beaded frame, and a border of rather nondescript ornament along the seat rail, possibly added later. In January 1930 it was published in its unaltered form (Robert Tasker Evans, *The Furniture Designs of William Kent*, THE ANTIQUARIAN, January [1930], p.45) as a sofa by William Kent. A few months later the same piece without its ornament was published in the Philadelphia Museum Bulletin (Joseph Downes, *A Sofa Designed by Robert Adam and Executed by John Linnell*, PHILADELPHIA MUSEUM BULLETIN, vol. xxv, No. 134, April [1930]) as an Adam design similar to the one attributed to Kent. The before and after were thus mistakenly believed to be two different pieces. To make things even more complex, there does seem to have been a second sofa making a pair. This was illustrated in Francis Lenygon's book, *The Decoration and Furniture of English Mansions During the Seventeenth and Eighteenth Centuries,* in 1909 when it was in the possession of Lenygon and Company. Comparison with the Philadelphia sofa before restoration reveals slight differences in the posture of the figures and in their drapery. The present ownership of this second sofa is unknown.

101. SOFA. Kedleston Hall, Derbyshire. Drawing Room.

H: 119cm; W: 363cm; D: 97cm. Carved and gilt wood, upholstered in pale blue floral damask. One of two different pairs of sofas, the other pair slightly smaller (W: 332cm.) with figures reclining back against the arm supports. Executed to designs by John Linnell, preserved in the album of his drawings in the Victoria and Albert Museum (92 D 26, E 124,129,131,138,139,140—1929). The inscription 'Lord Scarsdale's Sofa at Kedleston in Derbyshire' on one of Linnell's early sketches (92 D 26, E 124—1929) for this particular piece suggests a *post quem* date of April 1761. Linnell probably began the new project after 1762, the date of Adam's rejected proposal (fig. 98). Although Adam had no active part in the designing of these sofas, the influence of his, and Linnell's earlier designs for Lord Scarsdale can be seen in the gadrooned seat rail, the shape of the back, the medallion crest, and the use of mermaids and tritons as arm supports. On the other hand, Linnell, in making the figures free standing, in giving them horns and tambourines, and in decorating the arm supports with palm leaves, comes remarkably close to the lavish coach designed by Sir William Chambers in 1760 for the coronation of George III in 1762. The predominence of the palm motif in each of the sofas suggests that Linnell was also responsible for Lord Scarsdale's palm bed, mirrors, and torcheres. Whether Adam made any contribution to this Bedroom suite is unknown.

102. ARM CHAIR. Victoria and Albert Museum.

H: 106.7cm; W: 77.47cm; D: 63.5cm. Carved and gilt beechwood, upholstered in contemporary red floral damask. No design for the chair is known. It is, however, one of a set of four *en suite* with the sofa (fig. 103) designed in 1764 for Sir Laurence Dundas, 19 Arlington Street. The shape of these pieces and their rich naturalistic carving are characteristic of Adam's initial compromise between earlier forms and methods, and classical motifs.

103. SOFA. Formerly Mrs. Derek Fitzgerald, W: 243.8cm. Carved and gilt beechwood. *En suite* with the chair (fig. 102). Executed for Sir Laurence Dundas to a design dated 1764 (Soane Vol. 17, No. 74), and recorded in Adam's bill of charges for Arlington Street: 18 July 1765 'To a Design of sopha Chairs for the Salon £5.' (Bolton, II, p.345). Sold with three chairs at Sotheby's, 6 June 1947 (lot 154).

104. WINDOW STOOL. Formerly Walter P. Chrysler, Jr., New York.

W: 195.6cm. Carved mahogany, upholstered in modern green floral damask. One of a pair from a set of four originally in the Gallery at Croome Court. The stools correspond with an undated design for a 'Sopha for Sir Laurence Dundas' (Soane Vol. 17, No. 73), described in Adam's bill of 1766 for Moor Park as a '. . . Design of Scroll Stools for Salon £3 3s.' (Bolton, II, p.345). The design was presumably offered to Sir Laurence Dundas late in 1764 or in January 1765, but was rejected by him. It was then presented to Lord Coventry and appears among his bills from Adam: 'Feb. 1765. Another design of a Sopha or Scrol Chair.' The Croome stool is Adam's first fully Neo-classical seat furniture. Its round fluted legs, a feature far more common in France than in England, support the suggestion of French influence communicated to Adam in the crucial years 1763–5 by both Lord Coventry and Sir Laurence Dundas, fellow patrons of the Gobelins medallion tapestry.

105. WINDOW STOOL. Philadelphia Museum of Art.
H: 73cm; W: 147cm; D: 59cm. Carved and gilt wood, upholstered in Gobelins tapestry with floral bouquets on a grey imitation *damas cramoisy* ground. One of a pair *en suite* with six arm chairs, two sofas, and a screen, executed *c*. 1770 possibly by Samuel Norman for the Tapestry Room at Moor Park. The upholstery and the matching medallion tapestries were woven between 1765 and 1769 by Jacques Neilson. Like the related tapestry suites at Croome Court, Newby, and Osterley, the Moor Park furniture is often mistakenly attributed to Adam. The stool in particular has been associated with the one designed by Adam *c*. 1764 for Sir Laurence Dundas, and executed in the following year for the Earl of Coventry (fig. 104). Although the two are of a similar type having scrolled arms and straight legs, they are far too different in both size and detail to have been executed from the same design. There is no evidence whatsoever of Adam's participation in the tapestry suites. Nor is there any basis for Fiske Kimball's idea that through his designs for the Moor Park furniture, namely for this stool, Adam introduced the Neo-classical style to France. Not only are there no Adam designs for any of the pieces of tapestry furniture either at Croome, Newby, Osterley, or Moor Park, but there are also no bills as there are for his other designs. On the other hand, we know that the Gobelins' prospectus for the new medallion tapestry, drawn up in 1762, included matching furniture. Hence, it is more than likely that the idea, if not the basic design for the pieces came from France. The furniture was undoubtedly executed by English cabinet-makers who may also have been responsible for making the final designs and adjusting them to English tastes.

106. LYRE BACK CHAIR. Osterley Park, Middlesex. Dining Room.
H: 91.4cm; W: 52.1cm; D: 50.8cm. Carved mahogany mounted with a narrow gilt metal border around the seat upholstered in brown leather. One of a set of ten executed with slight modifications from an undated design (Soane Vol. 17, No. 93) inscribed 'Chair for Robert Child, Esq.' Although the chairs are usually dated *c*. 1775, it is more than likely that they were made *c*. 1767 by John Linnell, and are contemporary with the other furnishings which he supplied for the Osterley Dining Room. In Linnell's accounts for work at Shardeloes there is a bill dated 2 Oct. 1767 for '2 Mahogany elbow chairs with harp backs £5 10s.' This particular bill also includes a pedestal and urn (fig. 132) described by Linnell as resembling the one he had already executed for Osterley. It would appear therefore that similar designs were being executed simultaneously for both houses. Furthermore, a comparison of the chair with others of *c*. 1775 immediately reveals that it is of an earlier style. If dated 1767, the Osterley chairs would precede those designed and executed by Chippendale in 1768 for Rowland Winn at Nostell Priory

(fig. 107). The lyre back was one of England's major contributions to 18th century furniture design, and was later popular in France.

107. ARM CHAIR. Nostell Priory, Yorks. Library.

H: 96.5cm; W: 60.9cm; D: 50.8cm. Carved mahogany. One of a set of six supplied by Thomas Chippendale, and recorded in his bill of 22 January 1768: 'To 6 Mahogany Chairs with arms for the library the carving exceedingly rich in the antique taste the seats covered with Green Cloth £36.' Not only is there no documentary evidence of Adam's participation in the design, but a comparison with his Osterley model (fig. 106) reveals differences in the handling of the lyre, legs, seat rail, and total composition so foreign to his normal style as to be unquestionably the work of another designer—Chippendale.

108. ARM CHAIR. Osterley Park, Middlesex. Breakfast Room.

H: 88.9cm; W: 61.6cm; D: 53.3cm. Carved mahogany upholstered in pale blue floral damask. One of ten en suite with a sofa similarly covered, and with a simple fluted frame. The chair is patently influenced by Adam, but is not his design. It was probably designed and executed by John Linnell c. 1775–7.

109. ARM CHAIR. Osterley Park, Middlesex. Library.

H: 88.9cm; W: 62.9cm; D: 52cm. Veneered with rosewood, the splat and inlaid decoration of satinwood; mounted with ormolu medallion and swags. One of eight en suite

with two writing tables, and a large desk, combining the influence of Adam's Neoclassicism and of contemporary Louis XVI models, the latter especially apparent in the writing tables. Although the pieces are often attributed to Adam, there is no evidence of his participation, and the style is not characteristic of his work. Several variants of chairs with lyre splats and portrait medallions appear among the drawings of John Linnell in the Victoria and Albert Museum (92 D 26 E 63,95,108,336—1929). One in particular (E 336—1929 illustrated in Ward-Jackson, *English Furniture Designs of the 18th Century*, 1958. No. 243), a sketch in an elevation of a room, also includes the trefoil shaped back. The suite may well have been designed and executed c. 1775 by John Linnell. The chairs are a superb and unusual example of veneered and inlaid technique applied to seat furniture. The mounts, notably the medallion, bear comparison with those on the inlaid commodes in the Drawing Room. (fig. 45.)

110. 'SKETCH OF A HALL CHAIR FOR THE RT. HON. THE EARL OF COVENTRY.' Sir John Soane's Museum. Vol. 17, No. 92.

Pen and ink and grey wash. H: 34.8cm; W: 24cm. Inscribed with title and dated 1767. Probably for Lord Coventry's house in Piccadilly. The measurements of the chair are given as follows: legs 18in. high; seat 20in. wide, 16½in. deep, 2¾in. thick; back 23in. high, 17in. wide at the top, 15½in. at the base. The unusual back, formed of two scrolls surmounted by an anthemion crest, and joined by a crescent-like apron with a shaped and fluted splat, has no particular classical source but appears to be a combination of various motifs found on marble sarcophagi and thrones (e.g. Sedia Balnearia, Vatican Museum). The boldness of the design is characteristic of Adam's work at this moment, but this boldness disappears shortly afterwards.

111. 'STOOL FOR THE HALL AT SHELBURNE HOUSE.' Sir John Soane's Museum. Vol. 17, No. 76.

Pen and ink and grey wash. H: 40.2cm; W: 29cm. Inscribed with title and dated 1768. Based upon the porphyry tomb said to be that of Agrippa, in one of the niches under the portico of the Pantheon. The tomb was illustrated by Desgodetz in *Les Edifices Antiques de Rome,* 1682 (fig. 112). Adam had not only seen the tomb when he was in Rome, but he was also intimately familiar with Desgodetz's *Edifices*, which he had begun to edit and correct with the intention of presenting it as the trophy of his Roman sojourn. Although several fresh plates were engraved, the project was never completed. This design is one of the rare instances in Adam's work in which a specific source can be cited. The tomb was a particularly popular one, illustrated, for example, by Piranesi in the *Opere Varie,* 1750 (plate 6) and later by C. H. Tatham in his *Etchings of Ancient Ornamental Architecture,* 1799. (Pls. 94–5.) The stool may be one of the eight painted stools in the Hall listed in the 1806 sale of the furnishings of Lansdowne House.

112. PORPHYRY TOMB IN ONE OF THE NICHES UNDER THE PORTICO OF THE PANTHEON, ROME. Antoine Desgodetz. *Les Edifices Antiques de Rome,*

Paris, 1682. Plate V, p.19. Engraving from a drawing by Desgodetz. H: 32.5cm; W: 21.5cm. Detail.

113. 'SECTION OF A ROOM FOR SIR GEORGE COLEBROOKE.' Sir John Soane's Museum. Vol. 50, No. 54.

Pen and ink and water-colour. H: 50.8cm; W: 59.5cm. Inscribed with title. Undated, but *c.* 1771 contemporary with other designs for Colebrooke's house in Arlington Street. (figs. 42,87.) The sofa, a form of *turquoise,* is influenced by contemporary French models. The spiral fluted legs are of the type often found on Boulle furniture. The sides curved inwards, the back raised in stages, and the seat rail shaped. Richly ornamented and coloured red with gold detail. The niche similarly decorated with red and gilt ornament on a white wall. There is a rough uninscribed and undated sketch (Soane Vol. 6, No. 153) for a similar sofa. The piece was probably not executed. Figs. 66,114,115 are later modifications of this type of seat.

114. 'SOPHA FOR HIS GRACE THE DUKE OF BOLTON.' Sir John Soane's Museum. Vol. 17, No. 80.

Pen and ink and water-colour. H: 29cm; W: 42.9cm. Inscribed with title and dated 20 January 1773. This type of sofa with perfectly straight sides, although known in France at that date, is exceedingly rare in England where arm supports are normally curved or scrolled. Adam's use of the simpler form, together with small details like the foliated scroll finials over the arms, enhances the remarkably classical and elegant appearance of the piece. The unusual size of the sofa, according to the scale almost 10 feet long, suggests that it was designed for a position of special importance in one of the major rooms at Bolton House, Russell Square. Whether it was actually executed is not known. A sofa of almost identical form appears in Adam's section of the Northumberland House Drawing Room (fig. 66) also *c.* 1773.

115. 'SOPHA FOR THE RECESSES IN THE GREAT DRAWING ROOM AT LORD STANLEYS.'

Sir John Soane's Museum. Vol. 17, No. 81. Pen and ink and water-colour. H: 29cm; W: 40.3cm. Inscribed with title and dated 5 July 1774. A simplified and less interesting form of the straight sided sofa designed in the previous year for the Duke of Bolton. (fig. 114.) There are a few uninscribed designs for sofas of this description at Kedleston which probably date from the same period, *c.* 1773–4, and were presumably intended for Lord Scarsdale's house in Mansfield Street where Adam was working from 1772.

116. 'DESIGN OF A CHAIR FOR THE RIGHT HONBLE. LORD STANLEY.' Sir John Soane's Museum. Vol. 17, No. 94.

Pen and ink and water-colour. H: 43.3cm; W: 29cm. Inscribed with title and dated 19 January 1775. An arm chair in the Etruscan style with terracotta ornaments painted on a black ground. The splat and arm supports of scrolled acanthus, painted grey. Intended for Lord Stanley's bedroom as indicated on an undated pencil sketch (Soane Vol. 6, No. 155).

For other Etruscan furniture in Derby House see figs. 47,68,93,127.

117. ARM CHAIR. Osterley Park, Middlesex. Etruscan Dressing Room.

H: 90.8cm; W: 66.7cm; D: 50.8cm. Beechwood painted greenish grey with terracotta and black ornaments. One of eight executed to a design (Soane Vol. 17, No. 95) dated 6 March 1776. This design was chosen in preference to an earlier and more interesting one (Soane Vol. 17, No. 96, Box 1) of 25 January 1776 for a black chair with terracotta details and arms in the form of heraldic birds.

The present chairs are painted to match the walls and other decorations of the room (fig. 145).

118. 'SOPHA FOR THE EARL OF BATHURST.' Sir John Soane's Museum. Vol. 17, No. 82.

Pen and ink and water-colour. H: 24.5cm; W: 40.4cm. Inscribed with title and dated 18 April 1778. Probably for the Etruscan Room at Apsley House. A long bench fitted into a recess, and painted black with terracotta ornaments in the Etruscan style. The upholstered seat, the capitals, and feet coloured grey. Faint pencil inscription below giving directions to a draughtsman, 'Copy part of this Seat.'

119. 'HALL CHAIRS FOR SIR ABRAHAM HUME BART.' Sir John Soane's Museum. Vol. 17, No. 98.

Pen and ink. H: 29cm; W: 45cm. Inscribed with title and dated 28 March 1778. Alternative designs for hall chairs presumably for Sir Abraham Hume's house in Hill Street. Identical in form to a sketch dated 1774 for Lord Stanley (Soane Vol. 6, No. 157), but somewhat simplified in detail.

120. ARM CHAIR. Osterley Park, Middlesex, Tapestry Room.
H: 96.5cm; W: 90.2cm; D: 53.3cm. Carved and gilt wood. One of a set of eight *en suite* with a sofa, all upholstered in Gobelins tapestry, the backs with Boucher's *Enfants Jardiniers,* and the seats with floral bouquets on a rose *damas cramoisy* ground from designs by Maurice Jacques and Louis Tessier. The furniture coverings and the medallion wall tapestries were executed by Jacques Neilson 1775–6. Although the tapestries were ordered and woven for Robert Child, they were entered in Neilson's accounts as being for the King who supposedly, by this ruse, returned them to the Gobelins thereby discharging the debt of the *Batiments du Roi* to Neilson's *basse lisse* (horizontal loom) *atelier.* (cf. Letter from Neilson to Soufflot. 30 July 1776. Fenaille, Vol. IV, p.280). The Boucher *Enfants* are believed to be from the models executed for Madame Pompadour in 1751–3, which were immediately taken out of circulation and returned to Boucher. It was only after his death in 1770 that they were authorized for use. The scene illustrated here, *Petite Fille à la Cage,* is one of the few for which the model is still preserved at the Gobelins. The chairs themselves were probably executed late in 1776 when, or shortly before, the tapestries were received. Like the Croome Court, Moor Park, and Newby pieces they are intimately related to the medallion wall hangings but have nothing whatsoever to associate them with Adam. It can therefore be presumed that their basic design originated in France and was executed in England. This is corroborated by the rounded seat, a feature which is well known in France, for instance on *fauteuils à la*

Reine, but is rare in England where the slightly serpentined or shaped rail is normally preferred. The round fluted legs are also more characteristic of Louis XVI than English furniture. On the other hand, the splaying of the rear legs is a typically English custom not practised in France. It may not be mere coincidence that the medallion back was employed by Adam a year later, in 1777 for the Osterley Bedroom chairs (fig. 121), and again in 1779 for Sir Abraham Hume's chairs (fig. 122) which also feature the round seat rail. For Adam's furniture for the Osterley Tapestry Room see figs. 26,27, 138.

121. ARM CHAIR. Victoria and Albert Museum, and Osterley Park, Middlesex, Bedroom.
H: 100.9cm; W: 63.5cm; D: 55.9cm. Carved and gilt wood. One of six, two in the Victoria and Albert recently re-upholstered in pale blue striped silk, and four at Osterley in pea green silk. Executed from a design dated 24 April 1777 (Soane Vol. 17, No. 97). An elaboration upon the medallion back chairs made for the Osterley Tapestry Room *c.* 1775–6. The winged sphinxes, cleverly employed as back supports, reappear as acroteria on the projecting cornice of the bed (fig. 128), and as crest ornaments on the mirror frame (fig. 70). The design was modified in 1779 for Sir Abraham Hume (fig. 122).

122. 'DESIGN OF A CHAIR FOR SIR A HUME BART.' Sir John Soane's Museum. Vol. 17, No. 86 (Box 2).
Pen and ink and water-colour. H: 37cm; W: 17.4cm. Inscribed with title and dated

3 April 1779. One of a set for Sir Abraham Hume's house in Hill Street. There are two uninscribed sketches (Soane Vol. 6, Nos. 160, 162) for similar chairs. The design is an elaboration of the Osterley arm chairs of 1777 (fig. 121), with sphinxes flanking a small medallion, and pendant festoons carried up to frame the oval back. The legs with urn-shaped capitals are lighter and more elegant than those on the Osterley pieces. The upholstery pinkish yellow with red, blue, and green ornament. There are three coloured designs for the backs and seats. The first (Soane, Vol. 17, No. 89) for the 'Bottom of chairs for the second room. . .' 9 December 1778 coloured green, and 30 December 1778 coloured yellow. The second (Soane Vol. 17, No. 88 Box 2) 9 December 1778 for the 'Back of Chairs for the second room. . .' coloured green with a note dated 30 December 1778 'The back of Chairs for the first room in the same pattern as this but has a yellow ground as that of the bottom in the original drawing the white and red husks were kept more apart.' A third design 8 April 1779 (Soane Vol. 17, No. 90) is coloured yellow and inscribed 'Back of chairs for the great drawg [sic] room at Sir A. Humes in Hill Street. N.B. A drawing of the bottom was given to Mr. King but not copied being the same design as that for the other room only coloured like this.' Mr. King is probably of the firm of King and Pagget, upholsterers and cloth merchants from whom Sir Watkin Williams Wynne is known to have purchased fabrics in 1776. The upholstery designs suggest that the seat furniture of three rooms—the first and second Drawing Rooms, and the great Drawing Room—was to be covered with the same fabric in different colours. This fabric also appears on Adam's designs for a large sofa, a small sofa (fig. 123), and a *confident* (fig. 124) *en suite* with the chair. It is not clear whether these pieces were to be distributed between the three rooms, or whether the entire suite was to be repeated in each room. The former would seem more likely, but even then there would undoubtedly be some repetition particularly of the chairs.

123. SMALL SETTEE OR CONFIDENT. Formerly in the possession of Frank Partridge & Sons, Ltd.
W: 129.5cm. Carved and gilt wood, upholstered in modern red floral damask. One of a pair executed to a design dated 9 March 1780 (Soane Vol. 17, No. 85) for Sir Abraham Hume's house in Hill Street. The design differs only in having four rather than three front legs. The central leg is, however, a common feature of this type of seat for two persons—an enlargement of the arm chair, called a *confident* or *tête-à-tête*. There is also a design for a larger sofa of the same description (Soane Vol. 17, No. 84, Box 2). The small sofas are *en suite* with the larger one, the *confident* (fig. 124), and the arm chair (fig. 122). This pair of settees was sold at Christies 3 May 1923 (lot 102) by the 3rd Earl of Brownlow, the grandson and heir of Sir Abraham Hume. They then passed into the collection of the Duke of Roxburgh who sold them at Christies 31 May 1956 (lot 87).

124. 'DESIGN OF A CONFIDENT FOR SIR ABRAHAM HUME.' Sir John Soane's Museum. Vol. 17, No. 83 (Box 2).
Pen and ink and water-colour. H: 23.5cm; W: 44.5cm. Inscribed with title and dated

9 March 1780. A *confident* sofa, or a sofa with an additional seat at each end. The name and form are of French derivation as are details like the round tapered leg. This type of seat first appears in Adam's *oeuvre* *c*. 1773–4 in his section of the Northumberland House Drawing Room (Soane Vol. 39, No. 6). Although at that date the form was something of a novelty in England, by the 1780s it was quite popular. In 1788 Hepplewhite recommended the *confident* as an essential part of '. . . an elegant drawing-room with modern furniture.' (*The Cabinet-Maker and Upholsterer's Guide*, London, 1788, p.5). The piece is *en suite* with the chair and sofas designed for Hill Street (figs. 122,123). Its upholstery, like theirs, is of a pinkish yellow colour with red, blue, and green ornament.

BEDS

125. 'DESIGN OF A BED FOR THE EARL OF COVENTRY.' Sir John Soane's Museum. Vol. 17, No. 152.
Pen and ink. H: 40.2cm; W: 29cm. Inscribed with title. Undated but *c*. 1767. Adam's first finished design for a bed, the one for Their Majesties (Soane Vol. 17, No. 160) being incomplete. The design is neither a well integrated nor an especially imaginative one. It is not known to have been executed.

126. 'DESIGN OF A BED FOR THE RT. HONBLE FRED THYNNE.' Sir John Soane's Museum. Vol. 17, No. 153.
Pen and ink and water-colour. H: 43.1cm; W: 29.2cm. Inscribed with title and dated

1772. For the Hon. Frederick Thynne's house in Curzon Street. Other Adam designs for friezes and furnishings of the house 1771–3. Bolton attempts unconvincingly to relate the design to Queen Charlotte's bed at Hampton Court. Apart from a few faint similarities (the anthemion antefixes and parts of the ornament of the posts), which are common to most beds of this period, the two pieces are markedly different, Queen Charlotte's bed having no dome, and a straight cornice without the broken pediment, and urn.

127. 'DESIGN OF A BED FOR THE RIGHT HONORABLE LORD STANLEY.' Sir John Soane's Museum. Vol. 17, No. 154.
Pen and ink and water-colour. H: 52cm; W: 42.5cm. Inscribed with title and dated 7 September 17(74). An ingenious arrangement of two beds under a single domed canopy supported by palm tree columns. The whole is placed in an alcove fitted with draped curtains, the latter coloured blue with terracotta decoration. The bed and the wall behind are coloured beige with terracotta ornaments in the 'Etruscan' style. Although part of the date has been cut, it is established by the preparatory sketch (Soane Vol. 17, No. 155) dated 1774.

128. STATE BED. Osterley Park, Middlesex. Bedroom.
H: 457.2cm; W: 213.4cm; L: 259.1cm. Carved and gilt wood cornice on eight satinwood columns Japanned with black and green stripes and painted with lines of bell flowers. Inlaid plinths and chased gilt metal capitals. Dark green velvet curtains and valance both

embroidered, the latter with the Child arms on alternate tabs. The counterpane and interior of the dome of light green silk embroidered to Adam designs: that for the counterpane (Soane Vol. 17, No. 159) dated 19 August 1776, and for the interior of the dome (Soane Vol. 17, No. 158) 18 October 1776. The bed itself was first designed, 11 October 1776 (Soane Vol. 17, No. 156), with blue upholstery of somewhat different pattern, but was executed from a finished design of 16 May 1776 (Soane Vol. 17, No. 157). The gilded headboard, with a portrait medallion surmounted by dolphins and putti, and flanked by seated female figures, is reminiscent of designs by Neufforge. (Neufforge, *Recueil*. Vol. I, 1757, pls. 64,65,66.) The bed was criticized by Horace Walpole as '. . . too theatric and too like a modern head-dress, for round the outside of the dome are festoons of artificial flowers. What would Vitruvius think of a dome decorated by a milliner?' (H. W. to Rev. Wm. Mason. 1 July 1778. Toynbee Vol. X, p.282.) There is at Osterley (not on view; in the Taffeta Bedroom on the first floor) another Adam bed of simpler and less interesting form, executed in polished yellow wood with painted detail, from a design (Soane Vol. 17, No. 63) dated 10 April 1779.

129. 'ETRUSCAN ROOM AT LADY HOME'S.' Sir John Soane's Museum. Vol. 14, No. 132 (Box 1).
Pen and ink and water-colour. H: 32.2cm; W: 42.2cm. Inscribed with title. Undated but *c.* 1776. For 20 Portman Square. The bed, probably unexecuted, is a form of *lit à la polonaise* with the canopy supports concealed beneath the drapery. The upholstery

coloured beige with terracotta ornaments in the Etruscan style. The walls with similar decorations on a pale grey-blue ground, and the doors on a pale green ground. There is a rapid sketch (Soane Vol. 6, No. 110) with a head board similar to that on the Osterley bed (fig. 128) and a faint pencil inscription referring to Mr. Child.

PEDESTALS

130. PEDESTAL. Philadelphia Museum of Art.
H: 137.2cm. Carved and gilt wood ornamented on all four sides; the top of white marble. One of a pair from Croome Court. Although there is no design inscribed for Lord Coventry, there is one (Soane Vol. 54, No. 53) almost identical to the executed piece, entitled 'Pedestal for the Bust in the Temple of Bacchus for Mr. Hamilton' undated, but probably after 1761 the year of Adam's ceiling designs for the Temple at Pains Hill, Cobham, Surrey.

131. PEDESTAL. Victoria and Albert Museum.
H: 137.2cm; Side of base: 26.7cm. Pine painted white with carved and gilt ornaments on three sides. The plinth modern. One of a pair from a set of six designed for Sir Laurence Dundas, 19 Arlington Street. The design referred to in Adam's bill of 18 July 1765 'To a Design of Terms for the Salon £3 3s.' (Bolton II, p.345) is not in the Soane. There are, however, two related drawings of 'terms,' one for Sir John Astley of Patshull, Staffs. dated 1765 (Soane Vol. 17, No. 58), and the other of the same date

for Sir John Griffin Griffin (Soane Vol. 17, No. 59). The latter design was executed and is now at Audley End.

132. PEDESTAL AND URN. Osterley Park, Middlesex. Dining Room.
H: 152.4cm; Circumference of pedestal: 121.9cm. Carved wood painted white with gilt details; the masks and scroll handles of gilt brass. One of a pair executed by John Linnell before 2 October 1767 when they are described in his bill for similar urns and pedestals at Shardeloes (fig. 133). Although Adam's design is not preserved, the pieces appear with the sideboard (fig. 15) in the engraving published in *The Works*, Vol. III, (Pl. IX), erroneously labelled 'Furniture at Sion House.' Urns and pedestals are first introduced in the Kedleston sideboard composition of 1762 (fig. 3) which may also have been executed by Linnell. It is, however, with the Osterley composition that they emerge as single, free-standing units.

133. PEDESTAL AND URN. Dr. Campbell Golding.
H: 157.5cm; Top of pedestal 43.2cm square. Carved wood originally painted white, now stripped. The urn with foliage picked out in gold, and mounted with gilt brass masks and scroll handles. One of a pair from the Dining Room of Shardeloes. Executed by John Linnell whose bill, dated 2 October 1767, is preserved among the Drake papers (Buckinghamshire County Record Office, Aylesbury): 'To making and carving 2 coopers, the tops in the form of vases and large brass handles like Mr. Child's, one lin'd with lead to hold water, and the other Top sham and a pot cupboard underneath and painting the same all compleat. £30.' The urns and pedestals accompany a sideboard also made by Linnell (4 Sept. 1767 'To making and carving a large sideboard table with a mahogany top by drawing and painting the same £10 12s.'), and in the possession of Dr. Golding.

134. TRIPOD PEDESTAL. Sir John Soane's Museum. Vol. 6, No. 177.
Pencil and crayon. H: 25.9cm; W: 15.8cm. Inscribed 'Lord Coventry's (Tripod or Term?) for' with the words 'Water Stand' boldly written over. The sketch corresponds with one described in Adam's bill to Lord Coventry: '6 May 1767 A Tripod altered from a French design for a Water Stand £1 1s.' This provides conclusive evidence of Adam's knowledge and use of French Neo-classical designs communicated to him by Lord Coventry and other patrons. Although no French tripods of this date and description are known, it is not impossible that they did exist. In the rough drawing are the germs of the two finished designs for tripods published in the first volume of Adam's *Works* (figs. 135,136). The lighter pencil depicts a tripod supporting a vase candelabrum. The term figures appear to be joined by a fluted shell-like apron or basin with a central lion's mask. The darker crayon shows a closed water basin and a central shaft supporting a water pitcher. The figure on the left has a suggestion of horns indicating either a ram's head or a male grotesque.
The plan of the tripod is given on the right along with the measurement, 3 feet, not including the candelabrum.

135. 'DESIGN OF A TRIPOD WITH A VASE AND BRANCHES FOR THREE CANDLES.' *The Works in Architecture of Robert and James Adam.* Vol. I, No. 1, 1773. Plate VIII.
Engraved by B. Pastorini. H: 60cm; W: 45.2cm. Detail. Described in the text as a 'tripod for the Earl of Coventry executed in ormolu for Sir Laurence Dundass, and afterwards for the Duke of Bolton.' (*Works,* I, I, p.12) The tripod is closest to the part of the sketch (fig. 134) drawn in light pencil. The ram's head capitals are suggested in the horned head on the left. The putto mask replaces the lion, and the central shaft is continued up to support the basin. The design is peculiarly heavy, but more Roman in flavour than fig. 136. Of the two types, this was the less popular. These candlestands appear to be the first examples in England of a classical tripod translated into proper articles of furniture. Tripods had already been employed, however, by James Stuart before 1759 and by Adam *c.* 1761 (figs. 1,2, 3,6), as smaller ornamental objects.

136. 'DESIGN OF A TRIPOD AND VASE FOR CANDLES.' *The Works in Architecture of Robert and James Adam.* Vol. I, No. 1, 1773. Plate VIII.
Engraved by B. Pastorini. H: 60cm; W: 45.2cm. Detail. Described as a 'Tripod for the Earl of Coventry with a vase for candles.' (*Works,* I, I, p.12.) Presumably not executed. It is altered and refined from the darker parts of the sketch (fig. 134). The water basin is transformed into a decorative support for the vase candelabrum, and the pitcher is accordingly replaced by a classical urn. The design, although less interesting than the ram's head tripod (fig. 135), is more elegant and hence more indicative of the direction in which Adam was to move.

137. TRIPOD PEDESTAL. Alnwick Castle, Northumberland.
H: 123.2cm; W: top, 34.9cm; base, 45.7cm; D: top, 28.6cm. Carved and gilt wood. Identical to a design of a 'Tripod for the Drawing Room at Sir W. Wynne's in St. James's Square' dated 24 August 1773 (Soane Vol. 17, No. 60). The female figures may be to Zucchi's design, for among his bills to Sir Watkin Williams Wynne is one dated 26 September 1774 for 'Drawings for 2 figures in wood for Trypods £3.' (Wynnstay Mss. National Library of Wales, Aberystwyth). There are no designs or documents for the Alnwick pedestals. It is not known whether they came from 20 St. James's Square, or whether one design was executed for both Sir Watkin Williams Wynne and the Duke of Northumberland. Another tripod, identical except for the female figures, is illustrated in Margaret Jourdain's *English Furniture of the Later* 18*th Century* (Vol. IV, 1920, fig. 291) and was then in the possession of Geoffrey D. Hobson. These tripod pedestals are the forerunners of the one designed for Osterley in 1776 (fig. 138).

138. TRIPOD PEDESTAL. Osterley Park, Middlesex. Tapestry Room.
H: 127cm. Carved and gilt wood with painted medallions. One of a pair executed from a design dated 13 November 1776 (Soane Vol. 17, No. 62). The combination of painted, carved, and pierced ornaments is a departure from the usual pedestal types.

Although formed entirely of classical motifs, the piece has little resemblance to the classical tripods from which it was ultimately derived.

139. TRIPOD PEDESTAL. Victoria and Albert Museum.
H: 121.9cm; W: base 57.2cm; Diameter of top: 33cm. The upper half carved pine, the lower half carved Honduras mahogany with the swags, patera, and eagles applied. The whole painted egg shell blue with ivory white ornament. One of a pair from a set of four formerly in the Eating Room of 20 St. James's Square. The other two in the Melbourne Museum, Australia, are smaller and somewhat simpler. There are three related designs, two inscribed for Sir Watkin Williams Wynne and dated 26 April 1777 (Soane Vol. 6, Nos. 53,54); the third (Soane Vol. 6, No. 49), which is closest to the executed piece, is without date or inscription. The colour and ornament, particularly the ram's head motif, are repeated in the wall decorations and other furnishings of the room (fig. 25).

140. TRIPOD FOR THE NICHES IN THE FIRST DRAWING ROOM AT APSLEY HOUSE. Sir John Soane's Museum. Vol. 17, No. 64.
Pen and ink and water-colour. H: 25.5cm; W: 44.3cm. Inscribed with title and dated 16 January 1779. The low concave pedestal with animal supports is ultimately derived from a well known type of Roman altar. (See base fig. 77). But the richness of the antique models is entirely destroyed by Adam's restrained sophistication and effeminate pastel colouring, here pale blue with darker blue and off-white ornament.

141. PEDESTAL. Harewood House, Yorkshire.
H: 119.4cm; W: top 40.6cm square. Carved wood painted cream. One of a pair now in the main staircase hall at Harewood. Executed from a design (Soane Vol. 17, No. 66) dated 22 May 1779 for the Duke of Roxburgh's house in Grosvenor Square. Roxburgh House, altered, enlarged, and decorated by Adam between 1776 and 1780, was sold to the first Earl of Harewood in 1795 whereupon its name was changed to Harewood House. The house was occupied by the Earls of Harewood until 1894. It was probably at that date that the pedestals were removed to Yorkshire. The design may be regarded as an open or skeleton version of the basic pedestal form employed earlier (figs. 130,131).

142. URN AND PEDESTAL. Saltram House, Devonshire. Dining Room.
Urn—H: 80cm; Diameter of top 35.6cm. Pedestal—H: 83.8cm; W: 48.3cm. Total Height: 163.8cm. Carved wood painted pale green, cream and white with a figured medallion probably by Antonio Zucchi or Angelica Kauffmann. One of a pair executed from a coloured drawing (Soane Vol. 25, No. 159) inscribed 'Design of a vase and pedestal for the sideboard at Saltram,' and dated 23 November 1780. The urns are lined with zinc for use as wine coolers, and the pedestals are fitted as cupboards. *En suite* with the sideboard fig. 35.

143. DESIGN FOR A PEDESTAL. Sir John Soane's Museum. Vol. 17, No. 67.
Pen and ink. H: 42.7cm; W: 23.4cm. Inscribed 'For Henry Drummond, Esqr.' of

Great George Street, and dated 12 January 1781. The extreme simplicity and sleekness of the design are typical of the last phase of the Adam style. A comparison between this pedestal and the one of 1765 for Sir Laurence Dundas at Arlington Street (fig. 131) clearly illustrates the before and after of the Adam refining process.

144. TRIPOD POLE SCREEN. Osterley Park, Middlesex. Etruscan Dressing Room.
H: 167.6cm; Screen—H: 58.4cm; W: 52.7cm. The frame of carved wood painted greenish grey with black and terracotta ornament. The screen of embroidered silk. The tripod modified from a design (Soane Vol. 17, No. 148) inscribed 'Fire Screen for Mrs. Child,' and dated 30 April 1779. There are three designs (Soane Vol. 17, Nos. 141,142, 143) dated November and December 1776 for the screen, but the final one (Soane Vol. 17, No. 145) from which it was embroidered is dated 14 April 1777.

145. ETRUSCAN DRESSING ROOM. Osterley Park, Middlesex.
A view of the Etruscan Room illustrating the co-ordination between Adam's furniture and decoration. The room was condemned by Horace Walpole as 'a cold bath next to the bed chamber . . .' (Horace Walpole to Rev. W. Mason, 16 July 1778. Toynbee, Vol. X, p.282.) For the individual pieces of 'Etruscan' furniture see figs. 71,117,144.

*   *   *

146. MIRROR AND SIDE TABLE. Rijksmuseum, Amsterdam.
Mirror—H: total 363cm, crest 83cm; W: 176cm.
Table—H: 90cm; W: 180.5cm; D: 71cm.
Carved and gilt wood, the tables with semi-circular scagliola tops. One of a pair from the Drawing Room at Shardeloes. The date and authorship of the pieces are extremely problematic. No Adam designs are known, nor are the pieces listed in John Linnell's accounts for furniture executed for Shardeloes 1765–8. There is an undated design by Linnell, inscribed 'for the glass frames in Drawing Room at Shardeloes for Wm. Drake Esq.' (Victoria and Albert Museum. E. 241 —1929) which includes a similar scrolled acanthus crest with a larger central urn, and a bucranium below. Apart from these details, Linnell's design does not correspond with the executed piece. It is, of course, possible that there were later designs by him, now unknown. Mirror crests of this type also occur in several Adam designs c. 1768, but there is no exact parallel. The handling of the side panels, on the other hand, is not characteristic of Adam, and is suggestive of a later date towards the mid-1770s. The joining of the mirror and table is another late device which, with the exception of the Combe Bank design (fig. 57) of 1767, does not occur in Adam's work until c. 1775. The frieze and pendant ornaments of the table are quite close to an Adam design (at Osterley) for Robert Child in Berkeley Square, undated but contemporary with other furnishings for that house dated 1770–1. The legs, however,

are of slightly later style and of a type not employed by Adam. The pieces may be the result of the combined efforts of Adam and Linnell, or more likely Linnell's work incorporating earlier ideas of Adam's. Whether James Wyatt, who altered and redecorated parts of Shardeloes from 1775, had any hand in the design is purely conjectural.

147. OVERMANTEL MIRROR. Formerly No. 1 Bedford Square. Drawing Room.

Size unknown. Carved and gilt wood frame. *c*. 1779 possibly by Thomas Leverton to whom the interiors of the house are attributed. Both the mirror and the chimney piece are based upon Adam's design for Derby House (fig. 148) published in *The Works*, 1779. Thomas Leverton was one of the most frequent and skilful imitators of the Adam style.

148. 'CHIMNEY PIECE OF STATUARY MARBLE FOR THE THIRD DRAWING ROOM ORNAMENTED IN SCAGLIOLA & ORMOULU WITH THE GLASS FRAME OVER IT.' (Derby House, Grosvenor Square.) *The Works in Architecture of Robert and James Adam.* Vol. II, No. 1, 1779. Plate VI.

Engraved by J. Zucchi. H: 44cm; W: 58.5cm. Detail from a plate published 1777, and dated 1773. The mirror is also illustrated in the perspective view of the third Drawing Room (*Works*, Vol. II, No. 1, Plate V). It is described in the text as having been executed in 'wood gilt.' The design is not preserved, but it would probably be contemporary with other furnishings for the house, 1774 (the date 1773 on the plates referring to the starting of the house, rather than to its finishings).

149. MIRROR. Formerly in the possession of Mallett & Son.

Size unknown. Carved and gilt wood frame. A simplified imitation of the mirror (fig. 150) for Messrs. Adam at the Adelphi published in the first volume of *The Works*. The motifs, particularly in the crest, are fairly faithfully reproduced, but some have been added, omitted, or differently arranged thereby revealing the hand of a copyist.

150. 'DESIGN OF A GLASS AND COMMODE TABLE UPON WHICH IS PLACED A CLOCK AND VASES WITH BRANCHES FOR CANDLES.' *The Works in Architecture of Robert and James Adam.* Vol. I, No. 1, 1773. Plate VIII.

Engraved by B. Pastorini. H: 60cm; W: 45.2cm. Detail. Described in the text as 'executed for us in wood gilt.' (*Works*, I, I, p.12). The design for the mirror (Soane Vol. 20, No. 97) inscribed 'Glass frame for Messrs. Adam at the Adelphi,' and dated 1772. The table, for which there is no design, is of similar type to that for Luton (fig. 23). The shaped concave frieze is an unusual feature which does not occur elsewhere in Adam's work.

151. SIDEBOARD, PEDESTALS, URNS, and WINE COOLER. Harewood House, Yorkshire. Dining Room.

Sideboard—H: 90.2cm; W: 198.7cm; D: 81.9cm. Wine Cooler—H: 72.4cm; W: 76.2cm; D: 58.4cm. Pedestals and urns—H: 177.8cm (urn 88.9cm); W: 43.2cm; D: 43.2cm.
Carved rosewood inlaid with other woods and mounted with ormolu. The pieces are attributed to Thomas Chippendale *c*. 1772–5,

and are among the finest examples of English craftsmanship in the second half of the 18th century. Although it is often said that they were designed by Adam and executed by Chippendale, there is no evidence whatsoever of Adam's participation here, or in any of the Harewood furnishings. Furthermore, the handling of the legs, and especially the feet, the interpretation and spacing of the classical ornaments, and the general proportions and composition of each piece differ considerably from all known Adam designs. While the sideboard and its accompaniments are obviously indebted to Adam's style, they were not only executed, but also designed by another hand, possibly Chippendale's.

152. TRIPOD PEDESTAL AND CANDLE-STAND. Earl Spencer. Althorp, Northampton.

H: 190.5cm (pedestal 127cm; candle-stand from marble plinth 63.5cm); W: of pedestal 48.3cm. The pedestal of carved and gilt wood, the sides painted with winged female figures on a maroon ground. One of a pair designed by James Stuart c. 1759 for Spencer House, St. James's. The ormolu candlestands are similar to those in Stuart's sections of a Hall for Kedleston c. 1757 (fig. 1), and of the Painted Room at Spencer House, 1759 (fig. 2). They are identical to the one designed c. 1761 by Adam for Kedleston (fig. 3), and also executed as a perfume burner (fig. 6) for another Stuart patron, the Marquess of Rockingham at Wentworth Woodhouse. As they predate the opening of Matthew Boulton's Soho manufactory, they were probably not executed by him, but by another maker, perhaps Mr. Anderson

(cf. note to fig. 6). The pedestals, resembling those in Stuart's Kedleston design, are an example of the use of painted decoration on furniture.

153. PEDESTAL AND URN. Metropolitan Museum of Art, New York.

H: 167.6cm. Carved and inlaid mahogany. One of a pair, formerly in the collection of Sir George Cooper, Hursley Park, Hampshire. The designer and maker unknown. A comparison with the pedestals and urns designed for Kenwood c. 1768 and illustrated in *The Works,* 1774 (fig. a) reveals the influence of Adam's publication upon contemporary cabinet-makers.

154. PEDESTAL AND URN. Heveningham Hall, Suffolk. The Etruscan Room.

H: 96.5cm; W: top 71.1cm; base 43.2cm; D: 43.2cm. Carved wood painted pale green with terracotta and black ornaments in the Etruscan style, and fitted with metal candle branches. One of a pair designed by James Wyatt c. 1780-4, and probably painted by Biagio Rebecca who was responsible for other decorations in the house.

155. CABINET. Victoria & Albert Museum.

H: 355.6cm; W: 236.2cm; D: 68.6cm. Satinwood with marquetry of coloured wood, gilt metal mounts, and Wedgwood ware tablets. Designed by Mr. Crosse, and executed by Wright and Mansfield. Exhibited at the Paris Exhibition of 1867, where it was awarded the top honours.

The piece may be regarded as the formal inaugurator of the 19th century Adam revival. Wright and Mansfield continued to produce high-class pieces in the Adam style until *c.* 1886.

156. 'OCTAGON BOUDOIR — ADAM'S STYLE' by Messrs. Gillow. R. W. Edis, *Decoration and Furniture of Town Houses,* London, 1881, Plate 18.
Lithograph by Maurice B. Adams. H: 15.2cm; W: 10cm. Furniture and decoration by Messrs. Gillow, in the boudoir of the Princess of Wales Pavilion at the Paris Exhibition 1880. Mr. Edis describes the exhibit as 'an example of exceedingly delicate and graceful adaptation of eighteenth-century design to modern furniture; the panels of the various pieces formed in walnut-wood, with ebony inlaid, and laid over with box-wood, carved down, so as to show the ebony behind, in exquisite cameo-like medallions after Flaxman, the delicate enrichments and ornamentation of gilt lacquer-like character, were all elegant in design, and marvellously beautiful in workmanship.' (p.216.) The chairs and couch were of satinwood, upholstered with 'figured blue satin' which was also used to cover the large wall panels. The dividing pilasters were of maize silk with blue and gold decoration. The ceiling was ivory coloured with pale green enrichments, and the carpet was 'of rich Persian colouring on a maroon ground.'

INDEX TO PEOPLE AND HOUSES

Italic figures refer to Notes to plates, and bold figures to illustrations.

110

1. Detail of a Great Hall
at Kedleston. Attributed
to James Stuart, *c*. 1757.
Viscount Scarsdale.

2. Detail of the Painted
Room at Spencer House.
James Stuart, 1759.
British Museum.

3. Sideboard for Kedleston, 1762. *Viscount Scarsdale.*

4. Sideboard composition. *Kedleston Hall*.

5. Sideboard table. *Kedleston Hall.*

6. Perfume burner from Wentworth Woodhouse. *Victoria and Albert Museum.*

Design of a Table frame for the two Porphyry Tables — *End of the Table frame*

R. Adam Archt. 1765

7. Table for Sir Charles Farnaby, 1765. *Sir John Soane's Museum.*

8. Console table for Sir Laurence Dundas, 1765. *Formerly the Marquess of Zetland.*

9. Console table. Attributed to Thomas Chippendale, c. 1772–5. *Harewood House.*

10. Side table, 1765. *Syon House.*

11. Side table from Croome Court, 1765. *Philadelphia Museum of Art.*

12. Side table, 1765. *Syon House*.

13. Side table, *c*. 1765. *Syon House.*

Design of a Table frame for The Earl of Coventry

August 1767

14. Table for the Earl of Coventry, 1767. *Sir John Soane's Museum.*

15. Sideboard table, 1767.   *Osterley Park*.

16. Console table from Lansdowne House, 1768. *The Marquis of Lansdowne.*

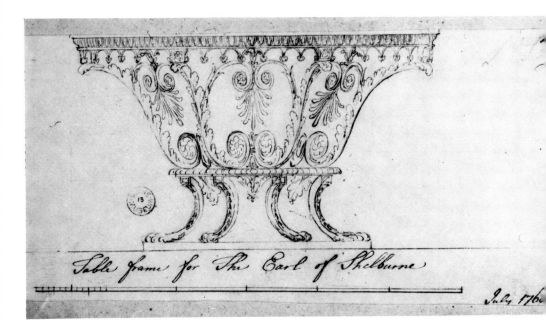

Table frame for The Earl of Shelburne

July 176[?]

17. Table for Lansdowne House, 1768. *Sir John Soane's Museum.*

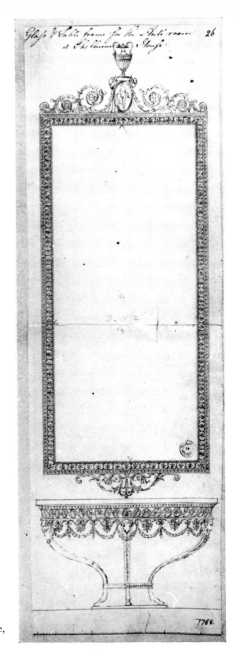

Glass & Table frame for the Anti room
at Shelburne House   26

1768.

18. Mirror and table for Lansdowne House,
    1768. *Sir John Soane's Museum.*

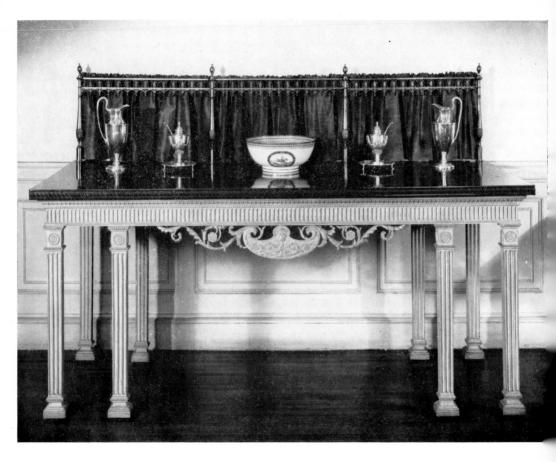

19. Sideboard table from Kenwood, *c.* 1768–9. *Ellery Sedgwick.*

20. Wine cooler from Kenwood, *c.* 1768–9. *The Wernher Collection.*

21. Mirror and
table, 1771–2
Saltram House

22. Mirror and table, 1769–71. *Saltram House.*

23. Table for Luton, 1772. *Sir John Soane's Museum.*

24. Side table from 20 St. James's Square, 1773. *Formerly C. F. Kindermann.*

25. Sideboard, pedestals and urns, from 20 St. James's Square, 1773. *Courtesy—National Museum of Wales.*

26. Side table, 1775. *Osterley Park.*

27. Table top, 1775. *Osterley Park.*

28. Pier table, 1775. *Nostell Priory.*

29. Pier table, 1775. *Nostell Priory.*

30. Table top, 1775. *Nostell Priory*.

For George Keate Esq[r].

Adelphi
1777

Scale of [scale bar]

31. Table for George Ke
1777. *Sir John Soane's Muse*

32. Side table, 1777. *Osterley Park*.

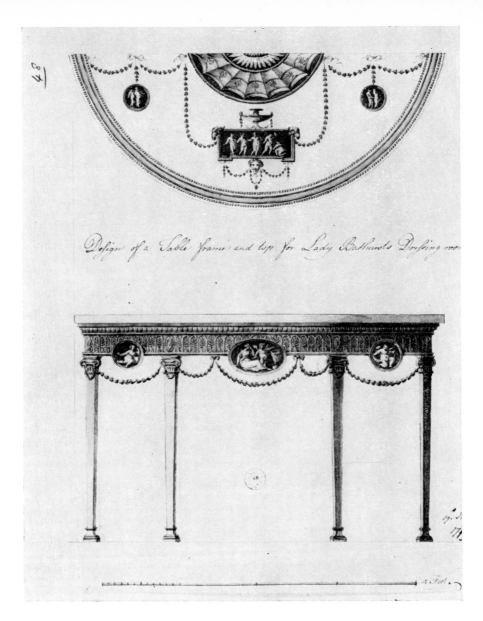

Design of a Table frame and top for Lady Bathurst's Dressing room

33. Table frame and top, for Apsley House, 1779. *Sir John Soane's Museum.*

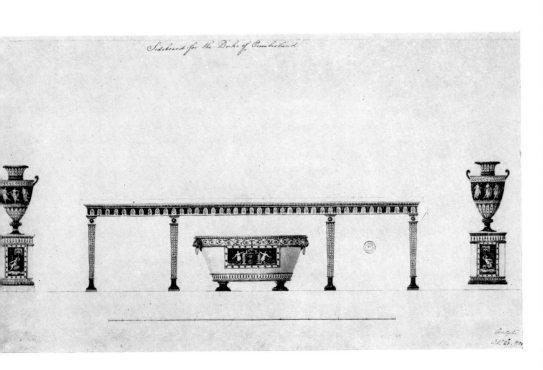

Sideboard for the Duke of Cumberland

34. Sideboard for the Duke of Cumberland, 1780. *Sir John Soane's Museum.*

35. Sideboard table, *c*. 1780.   *Saltram House.*

36. Table and
mirror, 1781.
Saltram House.

37. Clothes press from
Croome Court, 17•
Formerly the Earl
Craven.

38. Bookcase from Combe Bank, 1767. *Metropolitan Museum of Art, New York,
Cadwalader Fund 1917.*

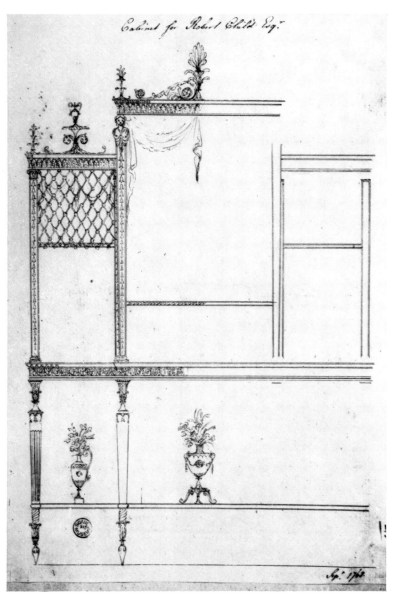

39. Cabinet for Rob Child, 1768. *Sir Jo Soane's Museum.*

Cabinets for the Room o...

40. Cabinet for Lansdowne House, 1770. *Sir John Soane's Museum.*

41. Cabinet from Kimbolton Castle, 1771. *Victoria and Albert Museum.*

Bookcase for Sir
orge Colebrooke, 1771.
John Soane's Museum.

Design of a Commode for Sir George Colebrooke Bart.

1771.

43. Commode for Sir George Colebrooke, 1771. *Sir John Soane's Museum.*

44. Commode for the Duke of Bolton, 1773. *Sir John Soane's Museum.*

45. Commode, *c.* 1773. *Osterley Park; photo—Victoria and Albert Museum.*

46. Japan commode. *Osterley Park; photo—Victoria and Albert Museum.*

Top of a Commode in the Countess of Derby's Dressing room　　*Dessus d'une Commode dans la Chambre à Toilette de Mad.ᵐᵉ la Comtesse de Derby*

Front of a Commode in the Countess of Derby's Dressing room　　*Facade d'une Commode dans la Chambre à Toilette de Mad.ᵐᵉ la Comtesse de Derby*

47. Commode for Derby House, 1774.　*R. & J. Adam, 'The Works.'*

Design of a Bookcase for Lady Wynn's Dressing room

3. Bookcase for 20 St. James's
Square, 1776. *Sir John Soane's
Museum.*

*Adelphi
3 Feby 1776*

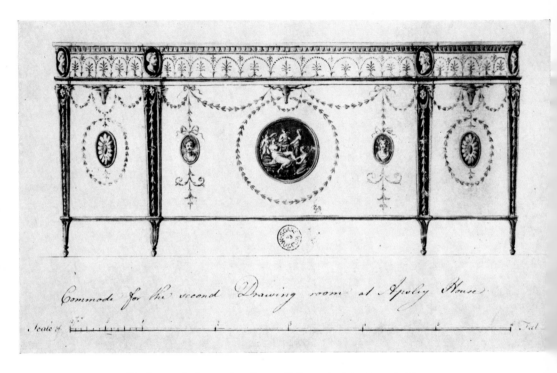

49. Commode for Apsley House, 1779. *Sir John Soane's Museum.*

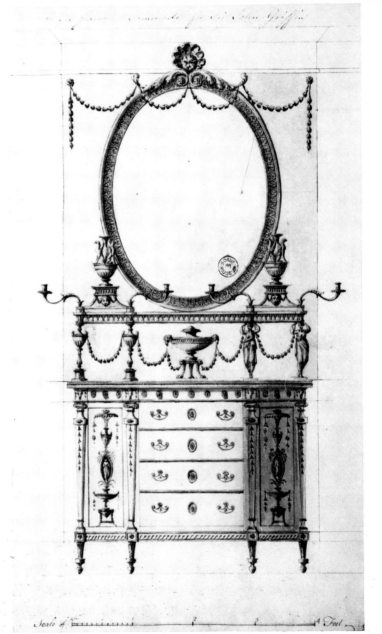

50. Mirror and commode for
Sir John Griffin Griffin, 1778.
Sir John Soane's Museum.

Scale of [feet] 1 2 3 4 Feet

51. Mirror and commode for George Keate,
    1778. *Sir John Soane's Museum.*

2. Mirror for the Earl of
Thanet. James Adam, 1764. *Sir
John Soane's Museum.*

53. Pier glass, 1765. *Syon House*

54. Pier glass, 1765. *Syon House.*

55. Pier glass, 1767. *Corsham Court.*

56. Pier glass, 1768. *Osterley Park.*

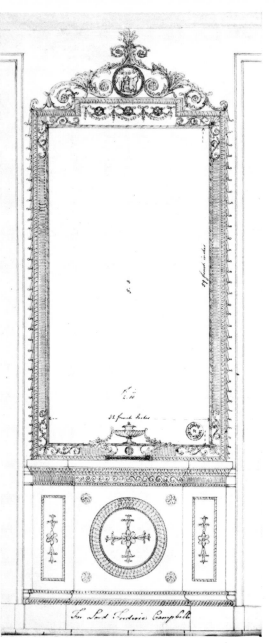

For Lord Frederic Campbell

57. Mirror and cabinet for Combe Ba[nk?]
1767. *Sir John Soane's Museum.*

58. Pier glass, *c.* 1767–8.
Kenwood.

59. Mirror and sofa for
Kenwood, *c.* 1767–9. *R*
& J. Adam, 'The Works.

Mirror for Newby, 1770. *Sir John Soane's Museum.*

61. Mirror, 1771
Corsham Court;
photo—
Country Life.

62. Mirror, table, and tripods for Luton, 1772. *R. & J. Adam, 'The Works.'*

Glass frame for the end of the Drawing room at Bolton House

Adelphi
22 Oct
R. W. 1772.

Scale of ...

63. Mirror for the Duke of Bolton, 1772. *Sir John Soane's Museum.*

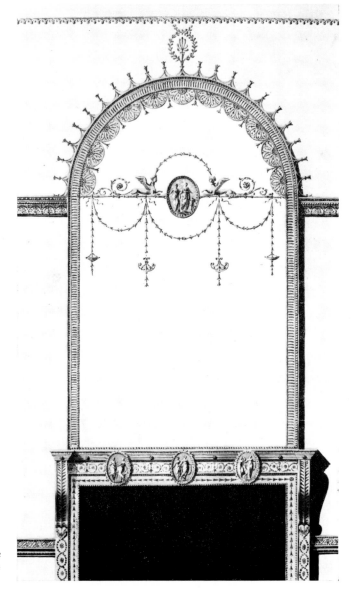

Overmantel mirror for the
rl of Harrington, c. 1773.
Sir John Soane's Museum.

65. Pier glass, 1773. *Osterley
Park.*

66. Drawing room for Northumberland House, *c.* 1773–4.　*Sir John Soane's Museum.*

67. Overmantel mirror fro
Northumberland House, c. 177
74. *Victoria & Albert Museu*

Chimney piece for the Countess of Derby's Etruscan Dressing room, of white Marble inlaid with Ornaments of Scagliola in the Etruscan taste, with the Glass frame over it.
Chambranle pour la Chambre Etrusque à Toilette de Madame la Comtesse de Derby de Marbre blanc marqueté avec ornemens de Scagliola dans le goût Etrusque, avec la Glace et sa Bordure au dessus.

68. Mirror and chimney piece Derby House, 1774. *R. & J. Adam, 'The Works.'*

Adelphi
25. Nov. 1774.

Glass Frame for the 2. Drawing Room at Ashburnham House —

69. Mirror for Ashburnham
House, 1774. Sir
Soane's Museum.

70. Pier glass, 1775. *Osterley Park.*

71. Pier glass, 1775. *Osterley Par*

72. Detail of the Music Room, Home House, 1775. *Sir John Scane's Museum.*

73. Mirror, Derby House, 1777. *R. & J. Adam, 'The Works.'*

74. Pier glass, 1777.
Osterley Park.

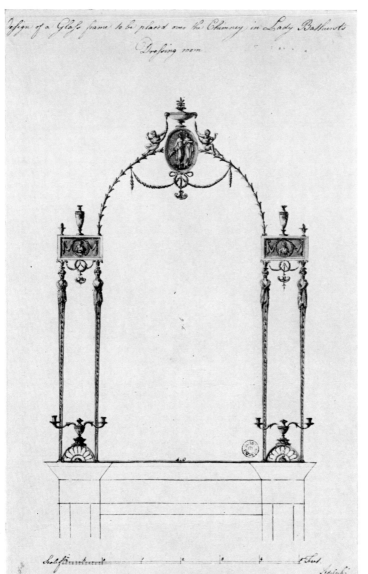

Design of a Glass frame to be placed over the Chimney in Lady Bathursts Dressing room

Scale of feet

Adelphi 31 Jany 1778

75. Overmantel mirror f[or]
Apsley House, 1778. *Sir Jo[hn*
Soane's Museum.

. Pier glass and pedes-
s for Apsley House,
78. *Sir John Soane's
Museum.*

77. Candelabrum. 2nd century A.D
Vatican Museum.

Pier glass and table for Sir Abraham
Iume, 1779. *Sir John Soane's Museum.*

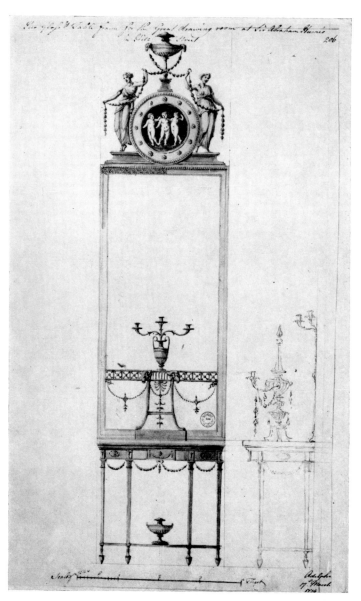

79. Pier glass and table for S
Abraham Hume, 1779. *Sir Jo'*
Soane's Museum.

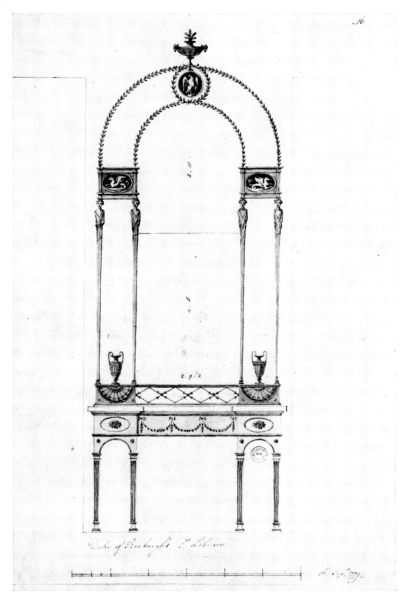

Mirror and table
Roxburgh House,
9. *Sir John Soane's
Museum.*

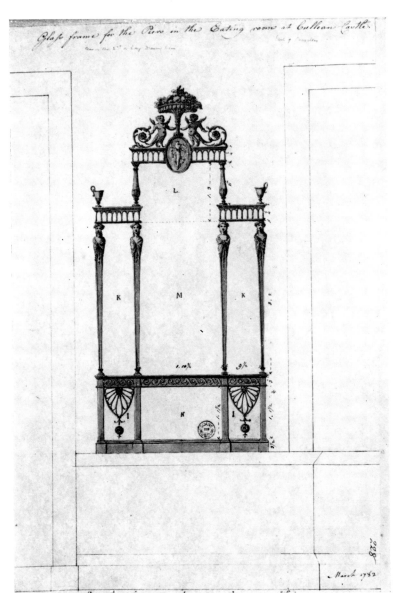

Glass frame for the Piers in the Eating room at Cullean Castle.

March 1782

81. Pier glass for Cu
Castle, 1782. *Sir
Soane's Museum*

82.   Mirror, 1765.   *Kedleston Hall.*

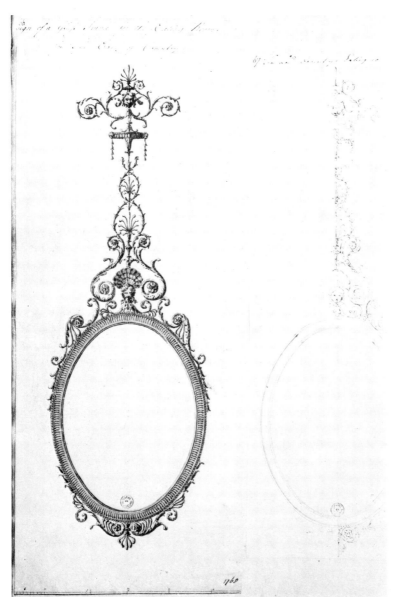

83. Mirror for the Earl
Coventry, 1768. *Sir Jo
Soane's Museum.*

Glass frame for Lady Coventry's Dressing room

1768

Mirror for Lady
Coventry, 1768.   *Sir
hn Soane's Museum.*

Glass frame for The Earl of Shelburne

85. Mirror for Lansdow
House, 1768. *Sir Jo*
Soane's Museum.

36. Girandole, 1770. *Osterley Park; photo—Victoria and Albert Museum.*

Toilet Table for Lady Colebrooke

1771.

87. Dressing tab
and mirror f
Lady Colebrook
1771. *Sir Jo.
Soane's Museum*

Pier Glass in
the Parlour

Glace dans les
Trumeaux du Parloir

88. Pier glass for
Kenwood, *c.* 1771-
2. *R. & J. Adam,*
'The Works.'

89. Mirror. *Former*
Mallett & Son.

90. Mirror for George Keate,
1772. *Sir John Soane's Museum.*

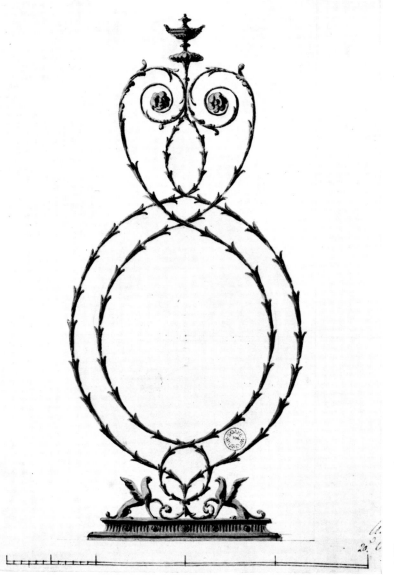

91. Mirror for George
Keate, 1772. *Sir John
Soane's Museum.*

Pier glass or girandole
Derby House, 1774. *Sir
John Soane's Museum.*

Pier Glass for the Anti room at Lord Stanleys in Grosᵛ Sq

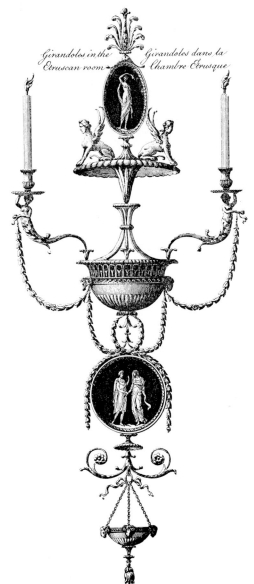

Girandoles in the Etruscan room — *Girandoles dans la Chambre Étrusque*

93. Girandole for Derby House, *c.* 1774. *R. & J. Adam, 'The Works.'*

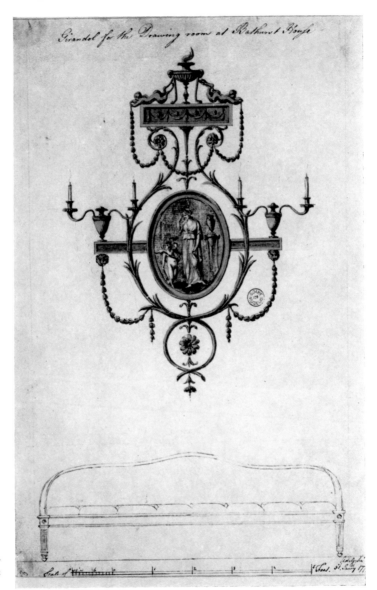

Girandol for the Drawing room at Bathurst House

74. Girandole for Apsley House, 1778. *Sir John Soane's Museum.*

95. Girandole for Ap
House, 1778. *Sir J*
Soane's Museum.

96. Arm chair, designed
c. 1761. *Alnwick Castle.*

97. Arm chair for Kedles
Hall. John Linnell, c. 1
Victoria & Albert Muse

98. Sofa for Kedleston Hall, 1762.   *Sir John Soane's Museum.*

99. Sofa. Anonymous. *Sir John Soane's Museum.*

100. Sofa. *Philadelphia Museum of Art.*

101. Sofa. John Linnell, *c.* 1762–3. *Kedleston Hall.*

2. Arm chair for Sir
Laurence Dundas, 1764.
Victoria and Albert
Museum.

103. Sofa for Sir Laurence Dundas, 1764. *Formerly Mrs. Derek Fitzgerald.*

104. Window stool from Croome Court, 1764–5. *Formerly Walter P. Chrysler.*

105. Window stool from Moor Park, *c.* 1770. *Designer unknown.*
Philadelphia Museum of Art.

206. Lyre-back chair, c.
1767. Osterley Park;
photo—Victoria & Albert
Museum.

107. Lyre-back arm chair
Thomas Chippendale,
1768. *Nostell Priory*.

8. Lyre-back arm chair. Attributed to John Linnell, *c.* 1775–7. *Osterley Park.*

109. Lyre-back a[r]
chair. Attributed
John Linnell, *c*. 17[.]
Osterley Park.

110. Hall chair for the Earl of
Coventry, 1767. *Sir John Soane's
Museum.*

Stool for the Hall at Shelburne House

111. Stool for Lansdow[n]
House, 1768. *Sir Jo[hn]
Soane's Museum.*

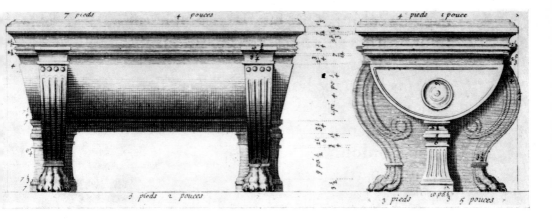

112. Tomb of Agrippa. Pantheon, Rome. *Desgodetz, 'Edifices Antiques de Rome' 1682.*

113. Sofa for Sir George Colebrooke, *c.* 1771. *Sir John Soane's Museum.*

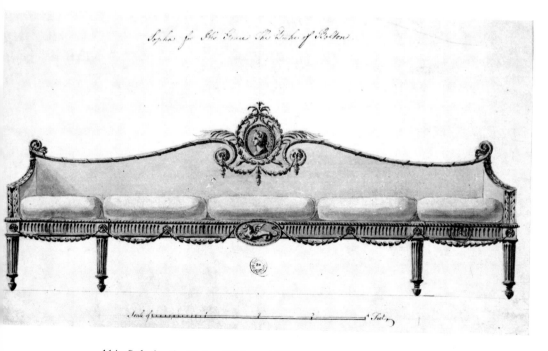

Sopha for His Grace The Duke of Bolton

114. Sofa for the Duke of Bolton, 1773. *Sir John Soane's Museum.*

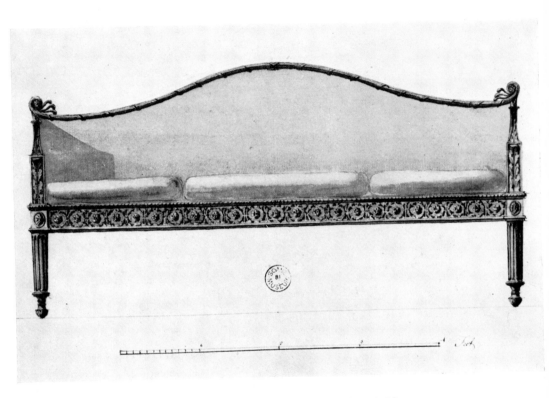

115. Sofa for Derby House, 1774. *Sir John Soane's Museum.*

Design of a Chair for The Right Honble Lord Stanley

117. Arm chair, 177
Osterley Park.

118. Sofa for Apsley House, 1778. *Sir John Soane's Museum.*

119. Hall chairs for Sir Abraham Hume, 1778. *Sir John Soane's Museum.*

120. Arm chair. Designer
unknown, *c.* 1776. Osterley
Park.

121. Arm chair from Osterley Park, 1777. *Victoria and
Albert Museum.*

Design of a Chair f. Sir A. Hume Bart.

86

Adelphi
3. April 1779

122. Arm chair for Sir Abraham
Hume, 1779.   *Sir John Soane's
Museum.*

123. Sofa for Sir Abraham Hume, 1780. *Formerly Frank Partridge & Sons Ltd.*

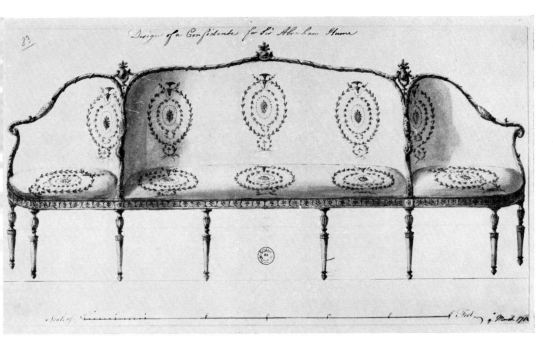

124. *Confident* for Sir Abraham Hume, 1780. *Sir John Soane's Museum.*

Design of a Bed for the Earl of Coventry

125. Bed for the Earl
Coventry, *c.* 1767. S
Soane's Museum.

Design of a Bed for The Rt. Hon.ble Hen. Frede. Thynne

1772

126. Bed for the Hon. F.
Thynne, 1772. *Sir John
Soane's Museum.*

127. Bed for Derby House, 1774. *Sir John Soane's Museum.*

128. Bed, 1776.
Osterley Park.

129. Bed for Home House, *c.* 1776. *Sir John Soane's Museum.*

130. Pedestal from Croome Court. *Phila-delphia Museum of Art.*

131. Pedestal for Sir Laurence Dundas, 1765. *Victoria and Albert Museum.*

132. Pedestal and urn, *c. 1767.*
Osterley Park.

133. Pedestal and urn from Shardeloes,
1767. *Dr. Campbell Golding.*

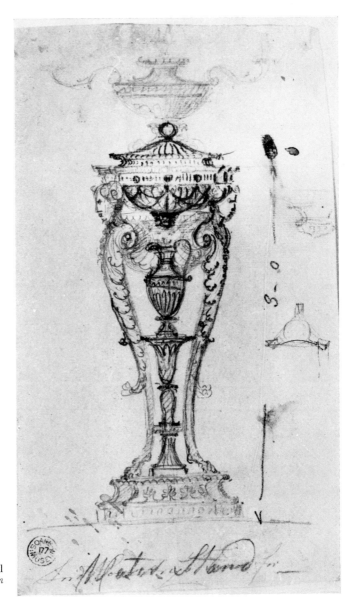

134. Tripod pedestal for the Earl of Coventry, 1767. *Sir John Soane's Museum.*

Design of a Tripod with a Vase and Branches for three Candles.
Dessein d'un tripié et d'un vase portant trois Chandelles.

135. Tripod pedestal. *R. & J. Adam, 'The Works.'*

136. Tripod pedestal. *R. & J. Adam, 'The Works.'*

137. Tripod pedestal, 1773. *Alnwick Castle.*

138. Tripod pedestal, 1776. *Osterley Park.*

139. Tripod pedestal from 20 St. James's Square, 1777. *Victoria and Albert Museum.*

Tripod for the Niches in the first Drawing room at Apsley House

140. Tripod pedestal for Apsley House, 1779. *Sir John Soane's Museum.*

141. Pedestal from Roxburgh House, 1779. *Harewood House.*

142. Pedestal and urn, 1780.
Saltram House.

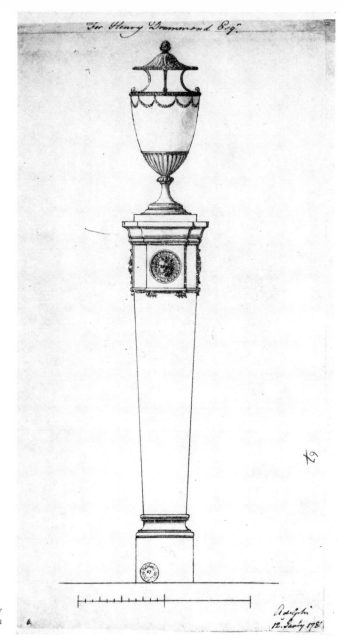

143. Pedestal for Henry
Drummond, 1781. *Sir John
Soane's Museum.*

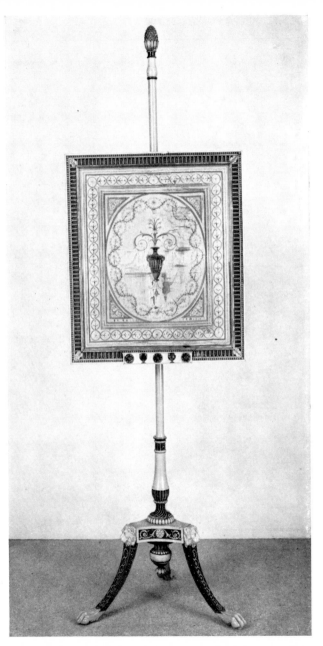

144. Pole screen, 1779 *Osterley Park.*

145. Etruscan Dressing Room. *Osterley Park*.

146. Mirror and side tab
from Shardeloes. Design
unknown. *Rijksmuseu*

147. Overmantel mirror. Attributed to Thomas Leverton, *c.* 1779. *Formerly No. 1 Bedford Square.*

Chimney piece of Statuary Marble for the third Drawing room, ornamented in Scagliola & Or Moulû,
with the Glass frame over it.
Chambrânle de Marbre Statuaire pour la troisième Salle d'Assemblée, orné en Scagliola et Or Moulû,
avec la Glace et sa Bordure au dessus.

Scale of

148. Mirror and chimney piece for
Derby House, *c*. 1774.   *R. & J.
Adam, 'The Works.'*

49. Mirror. *Formerly Mallett & Son.*

150. Mirror and table for Messrs. Adam,
Adelphi, 1772. *R. & J. Adam 'The Works.'*

151. Sideboard, pedestals, urns, and wine cooler. Attributed to Thomas Chippendale,
c. 1772–5. *Harewood House.*

152. Tripod pedestal and candle-stand from Spencer House. James Stuart. *Earl Spencer; photo—Country Life.*

153. Pedestal and urn.
*Metropolitan Museum of
Art.*

154. Pedestal and urn.
James Wyatt, *c.* 1780–4.
Heveningham Hall; photo—
Country Life.

155. Cabinet. Wright and Mansfield, 1867. *Victoria and Albert Museum.*

Octagon Boudoir · Adams · style · · Mefsrs Gillow ✳

156. Octagon boudoir
Adams style. Messrs. Gil-
low, 1880. *Lithograph*